CRITICAL INTELLECTUALS ON WRITING

CRITICAL INTELLECTUALS ON WRITING

edited by

Gary A. Olson
and
Lynn Worsham

STATE UNIVERSITY OF NEW YORK PRESS

Published by
State University of New York Press, Albany

Printed in the United States of America

For information, address State University of New York Press, 90
State Street, Suite 700, Albany, NY, 12207

Production by Diane Ganeles
Marketing by Fran Keneston

Library of Congress Cataloging-in-Publication Data
    Critical intellectuals on writing / edited by Gary A. Olson, Lynn Worsham
        p. cm.
    Includes bibliographical references and index.
    ISBN 0-7914-5841-5 (alk. paper)—ISBN 0-7914-5842-3 (pbk.: alk. paper)
    1. Authorship. 2. Intellectual life. 3. Intellectuals—Interviews.
    I. Olson, Gary A., date II. Worsham, Lynn, date.

PN149.C75 2003   2002042637
808'.02—dc21   CIP

Contents

Introduction

Stuart Hall writes about the "deadly seriousness" of intellectual work: "It is a deadly serious matter. I come back to the critical distinction between intellectual work and academic work: they overlap, they abut with one another, they feed off one another, the one provides you with the means to do the other. But they are not the same thing" (286). The distinction between intellectual work and academic work is an important one for those of us working in the academy. Simply stated, the distinction is this: academic work is inherently conservative inasmuch as it seeks, first, to fulfill the relatively narrow and policed goals and interests of a given discipline or profession and, second, to fulfill the increasingly corporatized mission of higher education; intellectual work, in contrast, is relentlessly critical, self-critical, and potentially revolutionary, for it aims to critique, change, and even destroy institutions, disciplines, and professions that rationalize exploitation, inequality, and injustice. Both academic work and intellectual work are political, though differently so. Certainly, academic work can become intellectual in the strong sense we have given it here, while intellectual work can lose its political vision and become merely academic.

It is within this context of the tension between academic and intellectual work that critical intellectuals must toil every day. Most work in the academy—academic and intellectual—is produced through writing, so we are all "writers"—at least in a superficial sense, if not in more profound ways. Writing—the production of

7

books, articles, reviews, and other such documents—is central to our collective work. Yet, any given scholar's relationship to writing is a uniquely personal one. *Critical Intellectuals on Writing* examines how twenty-seven of the world's most eminent scholars conceive their own relationship with writing and with the work of being a critical intellectual. For over a decade, *JAC*—a journal devoted to the study of rhetoric, discourse, and theoretical scholarship—has conducted extensive scholarly interviews with internationally renowned scholars from a wide array of intellectual disciplines. While these interviews concerned the entire extent of each interviewee's body of scholarship, each session began with a series of questions about the scholar's relationship to writing. *Critical Intellectuals on Writing* is a collection of excerpts from these interviews, specifically focusing on writing, writing habits and the work of the critical intellectual. Here, twenty-seven thinkers discuss whether they consider themselves to be writers, what their specific writing habits are, how writing relates to intellectual work, and the politics of intellectual work.

As might be expected, a group of thinkers as diverse as the ones here will have a range of reflections and judgments about writing, and each individual will have particular concerns central to his or her work. Judith Butler, for example, worries that the upsurge in anti-intellectualism in today's academy will have a negative and material effect on how intellectual work gets done. She has struggled all her life against the notion that intellectuals should strive in their scholarship to be "transparent" or "clear" because she believes such an ideal serves to shut down thought. She contends that rigorous intellectual work is necessarily extremely hard labor. Becoming a critical intellectual involves "working hard on difficult texts," and it entails "undergoing something painful and difficult: an estrangement from what is most familiar." It is precisely because intellectual work is so demanding, so painful, that many academics simply avoid it. Perhaps the very pain of intellectual work is one cause of the current increase of anti-intellectualism in the academy. For Butler, such anti-intellectualism is in part structural, in that people in the humanities are no longer certain that they are central to the academy;

they are derided by people outside of the humanities, and they are unable to articulate how their scholarship can have concrete effects both in the lives of their students and in the world in general. This anxiety often has disturbing consequences: "Those intellectuals who speak in a rarified way are being scapegoated, are being purged, are being denounced precisely because they represent a certain anxiety about everyone's effect—that is, what effect are *any* of us having, and what effect *can* we have?" While she agrees that those intellectuals who have a sense of social responsibility should be able to "shift registers," to work at various levels, and to communicate in various ways to various audiences, this does not mean that we should succumb to the drive toward transparency.

In fact, Butler is fascinated by the connection between difficult language and the opening up of new ways of understanding the world. She explains that having been formally trained in continental philosophy meant that she spent a considerable amount of time reading Hegel and Heidegger, and in both philosophers the difficulty of the language was in some ways indispensable to the philosophical views they were expressing. As a young college student, Butler was especially influenced by Heidegger's language, "his neologisms and his coinages." In Heidegger she found a "profound effort" to call into question "ordinary language and the ways in which we structure the world on its basis, an analysis of the kinds of occlusions or concealments that take place when we take ordinary language to be a true indicator of reality as it is and as it must be." Thus, in her formative years as an intellectual, she was "very much seduced" by the notion that "some newness of the world was going to be opened up through messing with grammar as it has been received." Such linguistic experimentation is, in Butler's view, important to critical thinking and to discovering new ways of conceiving the world. For Butler, being a critical intellectual means constantly interrogating our assumptions, continually calling things into question, not necessarily to do away with what is being questioned but, rather, to discover, for example, how terms might assume new meanings in new contexts. Such a stance means learning to "live in the anxiety of that questioning without closing it down too quickly." That is, true critical thinking is always accompanied by a certain unease: "anxiety accompanies something like the witnessing of new possibilities."

Given her faith in the generative capacity of linguistic experimentation, Butler is dismayed by the increased calls for scholarly work to be "accessible," to appeal to "common sense" through a "common language," and to be written within the terms of an "already accepted grammar": "What concerns me is that the critical relation to ordinary grammar has been lost in this call for radical accessibility. It's not that I'm in favor of difficulty for difficulty's sake; it's that I think there is a lot in ordinary language and in received grammar that constrains our thinking." Butler points out that accessible meaning, common sense, and the public sphere are all "fictions" that deceive us into believing that we all inhabit the same linguistic world. She finds it curious indeed that anyone would make such appeals at the beginning of the twenty-first century, given our "postmodern condition," given what we now know about language thanks to poststructuralist thinkers, and given the fact that we live at a time when there's "enormous conflict at the level of language." In fact, she comments that it is our social responsibility to accept the fact that "there is *no* common language anymore." This fact, says Butler, is "one of the most profound pedagogical problems of our time, if not one of the most profound political problems of our time."

Other scholars share Butler's concern about the increased anti-intellectualism in the academy and the attempt to erase certain kinds of intellectual work in the name of clarity and certainty. Jean-François Lyotard, for example, conceives of himself not as a writer but as a philosopher (because he must necessarily always be conscious of "meaning" when he writes), but he nonetheless sees writing (in the expanded contemporary sense of the term) as central to postmodern "openness" and resistance to certainty. For Lyotard, true writing is the attempt to resist "the network of exchanges in which cultural objects are commodities," to resist "the simple and naive exchangeability of things in our world." His conception of writing stands in contradistinction to the traditional notion of writing as an activity whose objective is to "master" a subject, to possess it, to pin it down. It is precisely this preoccupation with mastery, says Lyotard, that has impelled philosophy as a mode of discourse into "extreme crisis." The compulsion to master by erecting huge systems of answers, the search for a "constituting order" that gives meaning to the world, makes the philosopher a "secret accomplice" of the phallocrat. This is why he does not perceive his own writing to be "academic"; academic discourse entails what Lacan called "the discourse of the master," and Lyotard is not about to set himself up as a master, just a "perpetual student." Instead, what is needed in intellectual work is "perpetual displacement of questions" so that answering is never fully achieved. Since questions always already carry within them their own answers, are always interested, it is the act itself of questioning, of remaining open, that is most useful to Lyotard. And so, an "answer" is only interesting in so far as it offers a new question.

Thus, for example, philosophical inquiry about questions of gender is only useful when it is not attempting to stabilize gender categories or to end debate; such questions necessarily have no answers. In fact, Lyotard believes that our approach to questions of gender should be identical to how he conceives the act of writing—as questions posed without attempts to answer or master: "Maybe that's the best homage we can give to the gender question—'to write.'" Thus, attempts to associate masculinity with aggressiveness and femininity with passivity are "very very stupid." A more interesting issue is the relative "importance given to the body as such by both sexes." Philosophical—that is, male—discourse has tended to repress and externalize a "bodily way of thinking," to be suspicious of those who acknowledge emotions and bodily states, whereas women are "more sensitive" to these factors, according to Lyotard. What is needed, he suggests here and elsewhere, is to move away from a discourse of mastery and abstract cognition toward a way of being that recognizes affect, the body, and openness—a posture he defines as "feminine." Hence, Lyotard perceives a strong relationship" between "the ability to write in *this* sense and what I could call 'femininity' because there is a sort of openness to something unknown without any project to master it." For Lyotard, the opposite of a discourse of mastery is "passivity," the "ability to wait for, not to look at, but to wait for—for what, precisely, we don't know." This very refusal of the temptation to grasp, to master is for Lyotard "real femininity."

A former Marxist who devoted fifteen years of his life to grassroots socialist activism, Lyotard claims to have taken up writing and scholarly work as a kind of "mourning" brought on by the realization that "militant activity" was no longer effective. He is highly skeptical of organized resistance in general. Resistance, in the usual sense of "another policy or another politics," is not a viable alternative to the "system" because organized resistance, though sometimes necessary for checks and balances, eventually becomes absorbed into the system. True resistance, whether in social reform or another kind of reform, is up to each individual. True resistance is much like the capacity for people to "write," in the way that Lyotard uses the word. Thus, intellectual work, as Hall has said, is deadly serious.

Many of the scholars represented in this collection also see writing as a way to resist, as a form of political activism. Gloria Anzaldúa attempts to connect her writing to the "real-life, bodily experiences" of victims of various types of oppression; her intellectual work is an attempt to give voice to the silenced. Similarly, Chantal Mouffe sees intellectuals as those who provide a language for others to use to analyze, express, and transform their relations of subordination and oppression, and she feels a certain urgency about this deadly serious work because critical intellectuals—especially given the backlash from the political right—are facing a "big deficit" of transformative discourse: "There's a real lack of imagination on the point of view of left-thinking intellectuals in creating new vocabularies that will make possible a radical democratic hegemony." Avital Ronell sees herself as a kind of counterterrorist who calls for an "extremist writing" in an attempt to re-create the academy as "a sheltering place of unconditional hospitality for dissidence and insurrection, refutation and un-domesticatable explosions of thought." Ronell's extremist writing is reminiscent of

Donna Haraway's "cyborg writing," intellectual work that is "resolutely committed to foregrounding the apparatus of the production of its own authority, . . . insisting on a kind of double move, a foregrounding of the apparatus of the production of bodies, powers, meanings." Henry Giroux credits writing with helping define himself not as an academic but as a critical intellectual, someone who through writing has had the opportunity to exert influence in important public dialogues. Michael Eric Dyson also discusses the role of the public intellectual, claiming that writing has always been an important part of African American culture (despite its equally strong oral tradition), and insisting that writing continue to be seen as a central project of that culture.

These and the many other critical intellectuals represented in this collection together provide a lively, provocative, and insightful view of the role of writing in contemporary critical work. For the first time, twenty-seven of the world's greatest critical intellectuals appear in the pages of one volume to weigh in on the importance of a single topic. *Critical Intellectuals on Writing* serves as a unique and significant forum for these scholars to expound on their intellectual work.

Works Cited

Hall, Stuart. "Cultural Studies and its Theoretical Legacies." *Cultural Studies*. Ed. Lawrence Grossberg, Cary Nelson, and Paula A. Treichler. New York: Routledge, 1992. 277–86.

Gloria Anzaldúa

Q. Do you write at a regular time? Every day?

A. Not in terms of clock time, but in terms of my routine, because my internal clock changes. I get up later and go to bed earlier, and sometimes I write at night and sometimes I write during the day; but, yes, I have a certain routine. I get up, inject myself with insulin, and have my food. Generally, after that I have some activity like this interview. Or maybe two hours of filing and returning people's calls and letters—the stuff that I don't like to do. And then a walk, and then I dive into four, five, or six hours of this appointment with myself. Sometimes I can only do two or three hours, and other times I can do it around the clock. After writing, I take a break for lunch or the second meal, whenever that is. Then I do some reading, serious theoretical stuff, for maybe an hour or two, and then some escapist reading. I love mysteries and horror.

Q. What are some of your early memories of writing?

A. The whole activity of writing and the conditions that surround it as distinct from writing on a piece of paper started very early on orally with me: it started as a defense against my sister. When we

15

were growing up, we had to work after school: we had chores, we had field work, we had housework. Then it was time for bed, and I wouldn't get to do my reading. So I would read under the covers with a flashlight in bed with my sister. My brothers were in the same room, but my sister and I shared the same bed. And she was ready to tell my mom. To keep her entertained, and to keep her from going to my mom, I would tell her a story. I would make up a story—just something that had happened during the day—and I would make it like an adventure or a quest of the happenings of these little girls, my sister and myself, and, you know, I kind of embroidered it. So, she would settle down and go back to sleep and wouldn't tell my mom the next day. The following night she would want the same thing. Every night I learned to tell a little story. So I was writing stories very early.

And then this is what happened: she wanted two. So I got into doing serials. I would tell a part of the story and then break it off and say, "You know, if you don't tell, you'll get the rest of it tomorrow." It was like I turned the tables on her. So for me, writing has always been about narrative, about story; and it still is that way. Theory is a kind of narrative. Science—you know, physics—that's a narrative, that's a hit on reality. Anthropology has its narrative. Some are master narratives, and some are outsider narratives. There's that whole struggle in my writing between the dominant culture's traditional, conventional narratives about reality and about literature and about science and about life and about politics; and my other counter narratives as a *mestiza* growing up in this country, as an internal exile, as an inner exile, as a postcolonial person, because the Mexican race in the United States is a colonized people. My ancestors were living life on the border. The band was part of the state of Tamaulipas, Mexico, and then the U.S. bought it, bought half of Mexico, and so the Anzaldúas were split in half. The Anzaldúas with an accent, which is my family, were north of the border. The Anzalduas without an accent stayed on the other side of the border, and as the decades went by we lost connection with each other. So the Anzaldúas and the Anzalduas, originally from the same land, the state of Tamaulipas in the nation of Mexico, all of a sudden became strangers in our own land, foreigners in our own land. We were a colonized people who were not allowed to speak our language, whose ways of life were not valued in this country. Public education tried to erase all of that. So here I am now, a kind of international citizen whose life and privileges are not equal to the rights and privileges of ordinary, Anglo, white, Euro-American people. My narratives always take into account these other ethnicities, these other races, these other cultures, these other histories. There's always that kind of struggle.

Besides telling my sister these narratives, these stories, I started keeping a journal because my sister, my whole family is. . . . I don't know how to explain it. We would talk a lot and fight a lot and quarrel a lot. [As a family, we were] very verbal. In some ways like your average family in the U.S.: abusive verbally, or not aware of the vulnerabilities a child might have. So, I was always gotten after for being too curious, for reading. I was being selfish for studying and reading rather than doing housework. I was selfish because I wasn't helping the family by reading and writing. So anyway I had all of these emotions. I wanted to fight back and yell, and sometimes I did. But I would watch my sister have temper tantrums, and she would have temper tantrums so severe that she would pee in her pants. . . . She would get so upset, and I didn't want to be with her. I started shutting down emotions, but I had to find a release for all these feelings. I was feeling alienated from my family, and I was fighting against society—you know, your typical pre-adolescent and adolescent *angst*. So I started keeping a journal. I attribute my writing to my grandmothers, who used to tell stories. I copied them until I started telling my own, but I think it was my sister who forced me to find an outlet to communicate these feelings of hurt and confusion. So I started keeping journals. I have all of them lined up on top of my closet, but I think the earlier ones are still back home, so I'm going to try to hunt those up. I always keep journals, and I do both my little sketches and some texts. The pamphlet I gave you [which includes several drawings] came from a work-shop in Pantla that I did at the Villa Montalbo, a writer's residency right here in Saratoga. These people saw an essay that I had done about *Nepantla*, the in-between state that is so important in connecting a lot of issues—the border, the borderland, *Nepantla*. It was an essay I had done for a catalog, on border art as being the place that a lot of Chicanas do our work from—you know, the site of cultural production. These people wrote a grant and got some money, and so five of us (I got to pick some of the other artists) worked for five weeks on a project together and had an exhibit at the San Jose Latino Arts Center. My presentation was both textual and visual. I had the visual image and I had the text, and they exhibited them together on the wall.

So yes, if you define writing as any kind of scribble, any kind of trying to mark on the world, then you have the oral, the dance, the choreography, the performance art, the architecture—I had a feminist architect help me design this addition to my study. It's all marking. And some of us want to take those marks that are already getting inscribed in the world and redo them, either by erasing them or by pulling them apart, which involves deconstructive criticism. Pulling them apart is looking at how they are composed and what the relationship is between the frame and the rest of the world. In this country it's white. The dominant culture has the frame of reference. This is its territory, so any mark we make on it has to be made in relationship to the fact that they occupy the space. You can take any field of disciplinary study, like anthropol-ogy: that frame is also Euro-American, it's Western. Composition theory, that's very Euro-American. Thus, any of us that are trying to create change have to struggle with this vast territory that's very, very powerful when you try to impinge on it to try to make changes. It's kind of like a fish in the Pacific Ocean, with the analogy that the Pacific Ocean is the dominant field and the fish is this postcolonial, this feminist, or this queer, or whoever is trying to make changes. I think that before you can make any changes in composition studies, philosophy, or whatever it is, you have to have a certain awareness of the territory. You have to be familiar with it, and you have to be able to maneuver in it before you can say, "Here's an alternative model for this particular field, for its norms, for its rules and regulations, for its laws." And especially in composition these rules are very strict: creating a thesis sentence, having some kind of argument, having kind of a logical step-by-step progression, using certain methods like contrast or deductive versus inductive thinking, all the way back to Aristotle and Cicero with the seven parts of a composition.

So for anyone like me to make any changes or additions to the model takes a tremendous amount of energy, because you're this little fish going against the Pacific Ocean and you have to weigh the odds of succeeding with the goal that you have in mind. Say my goal is a liberatory goal: it's to create possibilities for people, to look at things in a different way so that they can act in their daily lives in a different way. It's like a freeing up, an emancipating. It's a feminist goal. But then I have to weigh things: okay, if I write in this style and I code-switch too much and I go into Spanglish too much and I do an associative kind of logical progression in a composition, am I going to lose those people that I want to affect, to change? Am I going to lose the respect of my peers—who are other writers and other artists and other academicians—when I change too much? When I change not only the style, but also the rhetoric, the way that this is done? Then I have to look at the young students in high school and in elementary school who are going to be my future readers, if my writing survives that long. I look at the young college students, especially those reading *Borderlands*. How much of it is a turn-off for them because it's too hard to access? I have to juggle and balance, make it a little hard for them so that they can stop and think, "You know, this is a text, this is not the same as life, this is a representation of life." Too often when people read something they take that to be the reality instead of the representation. I don't want to turn those students off. So how much do you push and how much do you accommodate and be in complicity with the dominant norm of whatever field it happens to be?

Q. Are there any things about writing that are particularly hard for you?

A. Yes, there are. I think one problem is for me to get into a piece of writing, whether it is theory, or a story, or a poem, or a children's book, or a journal entry. I am always rethinking and responding to something that I value, or rethinking somebody else's values. If the value is competition, then I start thinking about how when you compete, there is a certain amount of violence, a certain amount of struggle. Okay, behind that violence and that struggle I experience some kind of emotion: fear, hesitancy, sadness, depression because of the state of the world, whatever. In order to backtrack to the theoretical concepts, I have to start with the feeling. So I dig into the feeling and usually the feeling will have a visual side while I'm pulling it apart. One of the visuals that I use is Coyochauqui, the Aztec moon-goddess who was the first sacrificial victim. Her brother threw her down the temple stairs, and when she landed at the bottom she was dismembered. The act of writing for me is this kind of dismembering of everything that I am feeling, taking it apart to examine it and then reconstituting it or recomposing it again but in a new way. So that means I really have to get into the feeling—the anger, the anguish, the sadness, the frustration. I have to get into a heightened state, which I access sometimes by being very, very quiet and doing some deep breathing, or by some meditation, or by burning some incense, or whatever gets me in there. Sometimes I walk along the beach. So I access this state, I get all psyched up, and then I do the writing. I work four, five, six hours; and then I have to come off that. It is like a withdrawal. I have to leave that anger, leave that sadness, leave that compassion, whatever it is that I am feeling; I have to come off of that heightened, aware state. If I want to do some honest writing, I have to get into that state. If you want to do a mediocre job, you do a kind of disembodied writing which has nothing to do with your feelings or with your self or with what you care about. You care, maybe, only intellectually about putting out this essay so that your peers can respect you. So that is one problem of writing for me: engaging in an emotional way, and then disengaging. To disengage you have to take another walk, wash the dishes, go to the garden, talk on the telephone, just because it is too much. Your body cannot take it. So that is one problem.

There are other things that come up for me. One other problem is that you want to avoid that stage; you procrastinate. It takes you awhile to go to the computer. You circle around the stuff over and over. You do not want to get to the dissertation, to the master's thesis, to that paper that is due for this quarter, because you are going to be struggling with these things. That is the problem of avoidance, of not doing the work. Every day I have to recommit myself to the writing. It is like making a date with myself, having an appointment to do my writing. Some days I don't feel like meeting that appointment. It's too hard on my body, especially since I have diabetes; it takes out too much.

When I was at an artist's retreat for four weeks just last month, my computer broke down and I had to resort to handwriting. What happened was that I started writing poems. I had gone there to revise *Twenty-Four Stories*, which is a book I'm working on. I had taken nineteen of the stories in hard copy, so I was able to revise on paper, but the rest of the time I was doing poems and I was doing composition theory. I ended up doing a lot of stuff on composition theory. I also did work on a large book that I have in progress—the creative writing manual that I told you about. I did writing exercises for that book: some meditation, some hints and elements of writing, some fictive techniques. I didn't plan on doing any of that. I just wanted to do the stories, but not having a computer switched me over.

So anyway, those are two problems: the problem of engaging and disengaging, and the problem of avoidance. Then there is the problem of voice. How am I going to write the foreward for the encyclopedia I agreed to do? What voice, tone, am I going to take? How much can I get away with the Spanish? How much can I get away with the Spanglish? This is a pretty formal reference book. Another example is the bilingual series of children's books. How much can I get through the censors in the state of Texas in any particular children's book? The state of Texas has more stringent censorship rules than the other states, and most publishers can only do one book for all of the states. So the publishers tend to be conservative because they want to get their books into the schools. How much can I get away with pushing at the norms, at the conventions? That's another problem, and sometimes it's my biggest problem: if I can't find a voice, a style, a point of view, then nothing can get written. All you have are those notes, but you don't have a voice to speak the style. The style is the relationship between me, Gloria, the author; you, the person reading it, my audience, the world; and the text. So there are three of us. Or are there more than three of us? Well, in the author there is the outside author, there is the author who is the writer, and there is the narrative-voice author; and then in the reader there are all these different readers. And then the text changes according to the reader, because I think that the reader creates the text.

So I'm grappling with this voice and how much I can push in order to make people think a little bit differently, or to give them an emotional or intellectual experience when they can go and say, "Oh, so that's the Pacific Ocean?" Not quite that blatantly. Another example is Toni Morrison's *The Bluest Eye*. You never quite look at another black child without what you took from that text. It has changed your way of looking at black children. The problem of voice is the third problem.

I think another more external problem is one of censorship. With the very conservative path that this country has taken in terms of the arts, these times are hard. I know artists who can't exhibit nude photographs of their children because that's an obscenity. When you apply for the NEA or any other grants, you're limited. That's external censorship from the Right, of morality and family values. Then there is external censorship from my family: "Gloria don't write about that; that's a secret." You're not supposed to devalue Chicano culture. I was being disloyal to my mother and my culture because I was writing about poverty and abuse and gender oppression. So there's a kind of pressure on you *not* to write, not to do your art in as honest a way as possible. You're supposed to make nice, like you were talking about being Southern girls.

I write a lot about sexuality in my stories. I don't know if you read "Immaculate, Inviolate" in *Borderlands*, but when I sent my brother the book and he read it, he had a fit. He was going to show it to my uncle, and my uncle was going to sue me, because that was his mother I was talking about, my grandmother. I talked about how my grandfather lifted her skirt to do his thing, and how he had three other *mujeres con familia*. He would spend three days and three nights with my grandmother, and two days and two nights with the next mistress, and two days with the next one. The children from all the families played together, and my grandmother was ashamed of that and felt humiliated. I'm not supposed to write about that. I'm constantly asked by my family to choose my loyalty: when I choose who I'm going to be loyal to, myself or them, I'm supposed to choose them. I don't and I never have, and that's why I'm accused of betraying my culture, and that's why I'm a bad girl: selfish, disobedient, ungrateful.

To take the problem of censorship one step further, there is also internal censorship. I've internalized my mom's voice, the neoconservative right voice, the morality voice. I'm always fighting those voices.

Q. You collaborated with the artist on your children's book.

A. Well, it wasn't quite a straight collaboration, because I did the text first and then I gave it to the artist. But now I am doing a project for a middle-school girl readership, and there I will be working with the artist. But I also think that there is no such thing as a single author. I write my texts, but I borrow the ideas and images from other people. Sometimes I forget that I've borrowed them. I might read some phrase from a poem or fiction, and I like the way it describes the cold. Years and years go by, and I do something similar with my description, but I've forgotten that

I've gotten it somewhere else. Then I show my text in draft form to a lot of people for feedback: that's another level of co-creating with somebody. Then my readers do the same thing. They put all of their experience into the text and they change *Borderlands* into many different texts. It's different for every reader. It's not mine anymore.

Q. You don't feel possessive about your writing?

A. No, I don't; I've always felt that way about writing. I do the composing, but it's taken from little mosaics of other people's lives, other people's perceptions. I take all of these pieces and rearrange them. When I'm writing I always have the company of the reader. Sometimes I'm writing with my friends in mind, and sometimes I'm writing for people like you who teach writing. In writing, I'm just talking with you without your being here. This is where style comes in. Style is my relationship with you, how I decide what register of language to use, how much Spanglish, how much vernacular. It's all done in the company of others, while in solitude—which is a contradiction.

Q. Are there some stylists that have been important to you?

A. Well, I know that thematically Julio Cortazar has influenced me. He was an Argentinean writer living in France who wrote *Hopscotch* and *End of the Game and Other Stories,* and he wrote a lot about these in-between places of reality impinging on each other. In terms of my feminist ideas, my gender liberation ideas, *Jane Eyre* influenced me. I read it thirteen times when I was growing up. I really like how the little girl is so assertive. I like her being able to support herself differently from gender roles that were assigned to women. In terms of style, I recently read a mystery by Ruth Rendell, *No Night Is Too Long.* She writes popular stuff under the name Barbara Vine. She can really get into the rhythm of the lines, the words, the voice. I read Cormac McCarthy's *All the Pretty Horses*. I didn't finish the book, but I thought it had a style very similar to mine.

Style is a very difficult concept. Often I go to visuals to clarify my concepts, as I've said. For example, I think what's going on now at the turn of the century is exemplified by the *remolino*, the whirlwind, the vortex. North of the equator, the movement is clockwise, so all of our knowledge on this side moves clockwise. South of the equator, the movement is counter-clockwise. The rivers flow the other way here. As a *mestiza*, I'm living on the equator. Some of my culture, the indigenous and the Mexican culture, pulls me counter-clockwise. This comes with its own perception of being. And over here, in North America, all of the knowledge that I learned in school, all of the ways that I've learned to look at life, is pulling me the other way. I'm pulled in two different ways. I think that postcoloniality is situated right here. If you consider the counter-clockwise to be the colonized cultures and the clockwise to be the colonizer cultures, then there is this tension and you're trying to accommodate both of these cultures and still be comfortable. But it's a struggle to find this peace, this settlement. You have to change the clockwise movement to be counter-clockwise once in a while, and sometimes you have to change this counter-clockwise movement to move like the North. It's a state that's very unsettling. It's also the state you are in when you are trying to compose. Moving clockwise is everything that has been written: the literature, the norm, the genre laws. As a writer, you are trying to add to those genre laws, to that knowledge, to that literature, to that art. You have to go along with it in some ways, but to create some changes you have to go counter-clockwise. This is the struggle for a writer like me: how much can you get away with without losing the whole thing? All of these metaphors come around and around: to style, to composition itself, to identity, to the creation of knowledge, and to the creation of experience.

I think of style as trying to recover a childhood place where you code switch. If I am fictionalizing a certain experience, I go back to the reality of the experience in my memory, and it takes place in both languages. So I get into that style. But I think that what I was trying to do by code-switching was to inject some of my history and some of my identity into a text that white people were going to read or black people were going to read or Native American people were going to read. I was trying to make them stop and think. Code-switching jerks the reader out of his world and makes her think, "Oh, this is my world, this is another world, this is her world where she does this, where it's possible to say words in Spanish." It's like taking the counter-clockwise and injecting it into the clockwise. I think that's why I started that. And now a lot of Chicanas are doing it.

Q. Did you have any teachers that nurtured you in your writing?

A. One of the [high school] teachers that I had was really into building vocabulary. I remember opening dictionaries and ency-clopedias and reading whole chunks. I loved to look at the meanings of words. The whole time, I was very studious and very withdrawn from other people, very shy. That particular teacher said that I had a facility with words but that I needed to be trained. But then she would ignore me and pay attention to the white kids, so it was like a put-down rather than praise. Then I had a teacher in college who felt that one of the pieces I wrote should be published.

I went to grad school after I got my BA, and I had a teacher named James Sledd at the University of Texas. He was the first person ever to encourage me to talk about cultural stuff. I wrote an essay for him called "Growing up Chicana," which was the basis for the *Prieta* in *This Bridge Called My Back*. It was also the basis for a manuscript that I did on my memories, which I then took parts of and made into *Borderlands*. And now I have taken part of it and made it into a book of stories, and other segments of it are going into *la Llorona: Theorizing Identity, Knowledge, Composition*. All of that has its roots in the very first essay that I

wrote for James Sledd called "Growing up Chicana." He encouraged me to talk about cultural things, and I used some Mexican
words and some terms in Spanish. I had written some stories way
back when I was working on my BA, and some when I was
working on my MA. They all code-switched, but when I wrote for
James Sledd, we were doing something different. We were trying
to write formally: what we would call now theorizing; what was
then called criticism. His encouragement was very important to
me, and he was also very important to me as a role model. He was
very much a maverick against the university; he was very much at
odds, an outsider. From him I learned that an outsider is not just
somebody of a different skin; it could be somebody who's white,
who's usually an insider but who crosses back and forth between
outsider and insider. So he was my model to think about insider/
outsider, and then I had my whole life to think about *Nosotras*, us
and them. . . .

When I was working on my MA, I would constantly be marked
down on my papers for being too subjective, for not following the
rhetoric of Aristotle and Cicero—you know, the model that
people value, with the logical development of ideas. I would
constantly get marked down. Across the board, all of the professors—in Comp Lit, in English Lit, in all of the classes that I took
for my MA, and later on while working for a Ph.D. in Austin—
marked me down. Even the ones I took here at UC-Santa Cruz,
teachers who were using my book as a textbook—when I turned
in my papers, they would subtly want me to write the status-quo
way, even though they would use my book as a model for how to
do things differently.

So it was a great shock to me several years ago when the CCCC
conference invited me to speak. The very same discipline, the very
same teachers who had marked me down and had said that I was
writing incorrectly, all of a sudden invited me to speak. Then I
started getting requests for reprints in composition readers. That
was a shock to me. Finding that composition people were reading
me was a bigger shock than finding that anthropologists or that
women's studies people were reading me. . . . It was a big shock

for me to find composition people picking me up, and only a slightly smaller shock to find Spanish and Portuguese modern language people putting my stuff in their readers. Because we Chicanas were not part of Latino writing. They just included Mexican, South American, and Central American writers, not Chicanas. They put Sandra Cisneros in there; they put me in there. I am now a Latina writer. Can you believe that?

Q. It's very clear that you see writing and activism as related.

A. I think that a lot of the activism for writers and artists stems from trying to heal the wounds. You've been oppressed as a woman, or oppressed as a queer, or oppressed racially as a colonized person, and you want to deal with that oppression, with those wounds. Why did this happen to you? Why is it so hard? Who are these people that are oppressing you, and why do they have a license to oppress you? For me it started as a child. Children don't have any recourse. They can be abused by their parents. They don't have any rights. Society doesn't protect them. In my case, I was such a freak, such a strange little thing that I felt all of the ill winds that were blowing. I really felt them. I had a very low threshold of pain. The differences that I felt between me and other people were so excruciating. I felt like such a freak. I was trying to make meaning of my existence and my pain, and that in turn led me to writing. In writing I'm trying to write about these moments where I took things into my own hands and I said, "This is not the way things are supposed to be. Girl children are not supposed to be treated this way. Women are not supposed to be battered; they're not supposed to be second-class citizens. Chicanas shouldn't be treated in this way in society." I started grappling with those issues, and writing became a way of activism, a way of trying to make changes. But it wasn't enough just to sit and write and work on my computer. I had to connect the real-life, bodily experiences of people who were suffering because of some kind of oppression, or some kind of wound in their real lives, with what I was writing.

It wasn't a disembodied kind of writing. And because I am a
writer, voice—acquiring a voice, covering a voice, picking up a
voice, creating a voice—was important. And then you run into
this whole experience of unearthing, of discovering, of rediscov-
ering, of recreating voices that have been silenced, voices that
have been repressed, voices that have been made a secret. And not
just for me, but for other Chicanas. Look at all these women who
have certain realities that are similar to mine, but they don't
really see them. But when they read a text by Toni Morrison or
when they read *Borderlands,* they say, "Oh, that went on in my
life, but I didn't have the words to articulate it. You articulated
it for me, but it's really my experience." They see themselves
in the text. Reading these other voices gives them permission
to go out and acquire their own voices, to write in this way, to
become an activist by using Spanglish, or by code-switching.
And then they go out and they read the book to their little girls,
or their neighbor's kids, or to their girlfriend, or to their
boyfriend.

As with my children's book *la Llorona*, it's really very much
a cultural story. All that these Chicanitos read is white stuff, and
then along comes *la Llorona* and they say, "Yeah, my grandmother used to tell me stories like that." And it feels really good
for them to be in a book. There's this little kid—six, seven, eight,
nine, ten—who never sees himself represented, so unearthing and
nurturing that voice is part of the activism work. That's why I try
to do so many anthologies. That's why I promote women, especially women of color and lesbians of all colors, and why I'm on
editorial boards for magazines: because I want to get their voices
out there. I believe that says something about activism, because in
the process of creating the composition, the work of art, the
painting, the film, you're creating the culture. You're rewriting
the culture, which is very much an activist kind of thing. So
writers have something in common with all of these people doing
grassroots organizing and acting in the community: it's all about
rewriting culture. You don't want a culture that batters women
and children. By the year 2005, fifty percent of the group that is

going to be labeled "poverty stricken"—fifty percent of it—are going to be women and children. That's a whole new thing, women out of jobs, homeless children. It's a reality that we need to speak of. Twenty years ago, incest was not part of consensual reality. It was the writers who wrote about it, feminists who talked about it, who made films about it, and who did art about incest and child abuse, who changed reality. Before that, it was just a given. You beat your wife, that's part of it. Having abusive sex with your wife is not rape. Consensual reality has been redefined by these people rewriting a culture. Now it's part of culture that when you batter someone, you're supposed to be responsible. It's not something you can get away with unless you're a psychopath.

❦ ❦ ❦

Mary Field Belenky

Q. Do you think of yourself as a writer?

A. I do, and I'm very puzzled by it because I find writing so hard, so arduous, so painful. If you're engaged as I am in research that's embedded in interpretive-descriptive processes, your major research tool is trying to articulate clearly the understandings that you're coming to—and writing is integral to this process. Interpretive-descriptive research is very different from traditional research in the social sciences, which relies on statistical tools to communicate findings. In the research that my colleagues and I do, we're following in the steps of such social scientists as Piaget, Perry, Kohlberg, and Gilligan. They are all writing a story that grows out of conversation, and they savor the words of the people they've been interviewing, putting the words in a story line. The goal of their work is to understand and describe people's thinking, to try to understand the structures of mind, so the only tool they have is language: language for eliciting people's thoughts, language for trying to understand the deep organizing principles of thought, and, finally, language for articulating these things. So narrative has become a particularly important tool for social scientists who are trying to understand thinking. You know, Lawrence Kohlberg once told me that when he was conducting moral judgment studies at Yale in the late 1950s, several people asked him why he spent his time looking at verbal behavior. It has taken psychology a long time to notice that humans are meaning-making animals.

Q. Would you describe how you and your colleagues researched and wrote *Women's Ways of Knowing* collaboratively?

A. We had the first of what we came to call our "pajama-party" meetings at a motel in New Hampshire that was a midway point from where we all were living. In our conversations there, we kept going around and around, trying to articulate what our driving questions were and, also, what we perceived as the driving questions at the edge of our discipline. After this period of eating, swimming, and talking, we went home, wrote a proposal, and got funding from FIPSE. What we created at this first pajama party was an umbrella that framed most of our important questions, even though they were still vague.

Because we all lived in different places, the grant gave us financial support to hold one of these pajama-party meetings about every five weeks for three years. Very regularly, then, every five or six weeks, we were able to sit down together and work around the clock for three or four days at a time. I can't tell you how important it is to have this kind of time for working, sleeping on your thoughts, and returning to the conversation—without distractions from children and telephones. We all had raised families as well as having careers, and the luxury of that kind of sustained conversation was just terrific. The pajama party was very important to the process.

During the three-year period that FIPSE funded us, we developed a very broad conversation with women from all walks of life. . . . In the process of carrying out FIPSE's goals, however, we collected these marvelous interviews and had them transcribed. We were very much interested in the research questions, and working with the faculty on this development project brought a whole other group of people into the conversation. Our work was enriched because it was cast as an *action* project rather than just research.

The women we interviewed were themselves drawn in. A word that seems better than *collaboration* is *dialogue* because it suggests that our so-called research subjects were real participants in the project. In a very real sense they were also, much of the time when we were writing, the audience. Let me tell you about Lillian Rubin's *Worlds of Pain*, a study of lower middle-class marriages—a study that is, like ours, based on interviews. Rubin had a pact with the people that she interviewed: they would review and approve any writing she did before it went to publication. She notes that none of those people had much criticism of her writing, so she didn't change or reedit the work in light of it; but I believe, because she had this pact to give them the work before publishing it, that she wrote *to them* in a way—and it's a beautiful book. Rubin's book was a model for us, even though our sample was too large to promise everybody we would get their permission. But as our book was written, we very much had in mind that it would be read by the people we had interviewed.

The information wasn't just what *we* were thinking or organizing; it was also *their* words because we worked from transcripts of the interviews. In fact, when the book first came out many women said that we had given words to things they'd always thought. It seemed funny at first, a backhanded kind of compliment. Here we'd done this extraordinary thing. But giving words to these ideas was exactly what we tried to do, and that's a lot to do. Moreover, I think we ought to teach ourselves and our students that we can have real choices about audience. We all need to understand how writing the same material for different audiences changes the voice. That is very empowering knowledge to have.

Q. How did you coordinate the writing of the book?

A. We had a month-long pajama party at a cottage on the shore, a big rambling mansion on the ocean. We spent the month trying to frame the book and talking through the process of writing it; by the end of the month, we had a reasonably firm view of its shape, so we sketched out a table of contents. Then when we looked at the plan, it made sense that one person or another would write certain chapters. Certainly, some decisions were arbitrary, but for the most part we saw a clear and rational division of labor that made deep sense. We also made a decision that in retrospect I think was very smart: that we would not put our names on different pieces. I don't know why we made that decision, and I'm still not sure why that was so smart. But I think it was, and it's probably one of the reasons the book ultimately developed the one-voice quality that it has.

We all got computerized early on, but we made a decision to send hard copy—and I think that's very important. I wouldn't want to send around disks and have people start changing the text. So we sent around drafts and we wrote all over them. On the whole, we were amazingly excited and loving of what went around and amazingly hard-nosed and critical. We said, "Does that really make sense?" and "Say more," and "Why would you say that?" and "Where's your evidence?" For the most part even the early drafts were interesting. It was exciting to get the chapters, and we worked very hard criticizing them.

We would each get the hard copy back, three copies with lots of writing all over the margins, and we would choose whether to follow the suggestions. If you send your disk around and people start changing it, your words and theirs get merged too fast; you need some sort of a balance. Writing collaboratively gets very confusing because, when you're really working together, when the dialogue really starts, ideas grow and change and no one has real ownership. Yet you have to keep, or you ought to keep, your own voice. Having comments on paper is wonderful because you keep all of the different voices separate for a while. Because of the way my colleagues each wrote in the margin, I always knew their handwriting, and so as I worked on redrafting I had their different voices to work with.

At times someone would write something so gorgeous that you would think it needed to be in your own chapter and you'd fight for it. Sometimes I found myself winning one of those fights and integrating into my own text a beautiful perception from someone else's text, their words and my words. This process is really very sensuous. It's so loving to have that mingling going on—knowing that these are stolen words in a way, words coaxed out of someone, but liking the closeness of having her words and my words all mingling right in there. Sometimes this feeling happened, too, as we worked with the interviews that we had collected from the women. I'm sure others have experienced this—for example, when they're putting a beloved mentor's words in a document that they're working on. In my teaching, I try to get students to cite a text and put that scholar's words and name next to their own words and name, and I try to help them understand that this is a way of making it clear that the two of them are talking together now.

The book could not have been written by any single one of us, without this broader conversation. It has a scope that reflects a wide range of experiences in a wide range of institutions, and a single person couldn't have created that. I don't think a single person can get the kind of clarity that comes through working together to pull away the chaff and let the bold ideas come forth.

Q. People discussing coauthored works such as *Women's Ways* don't seem to have a conventional way to refer to collective authors. For example, they often refer to *you* as the author of this study, thus unwittingly diminishing the contributions of your colleagues. Do you have any solutions to this dilemma?

A. This is a serious problem. The people who've had the most interesting things to say about our work are also people who have figured out gracious ways of acknowledging its collaborative nature. Sometimes they've solved the problem in very conventional ways, like writing out all the names each time. Now, that sounds awkward, but when you're reading it's just a clump of text that registers the same way a single name does. Or they find another way of referring to us, saying, "the authors of *Women's Ways*" or "the collaborative" or "the research group." They never single out one person. We have to learn, and we have to find forms for naming collective authors or collaboration is not going to become routine. I suspect that we will find forms as constructive knowledge becomes more widely disseminated in the culture, more widely valued, as more and more we see that this is how our children have to be educated to become constructors of knowledge, as we learn to value the collaborative process. Sooner or later we're going to find forums to support and cultivate collaboration, and then we'll cut across all disciplines.

In the academy, collaborative work is demoted, but it should count *double* in faculty evaluations. If a work is embedded in a collaborative process, the writers goad each other into endless revisions. For example, in our study there's hardly a page that wasn't rewritten fifteen or twenty times. No one working alone can do that kind of intensive revision, nor can they benefit from the extensive redrafting that takes place in conversation. The kind of reflection and revising enabled by collaboration brings a quality of depth and scope to a work. Collaborating may only produce two-hundred or three-hundred pages of text, but perhaps they're more enduring than the two- or three-hundred pages of a single voice.

❦ ❦ ❦

Homi Bhabha

Q. Do you consider yourself to be a writer?

A. Yes, very much so. In fact, when I was an undergraduate at the University of Bombay, it always surprised me how completely absorbed I would be when I wrote my rather small and worthless poems. I was entirely enchanted by the form and the activity. Somehow the agony in "creative writing" (as they call it) seemed much sweeter than the agony in theoretical writing. It just surprised me how completely absorbing it was to decide to use one word rather than another. I wrote rather short poems; that was the form I worked in. The consequence of this for my present work is that I'm very fascinated by doing theory *by* doing a certain kind of writing. To me, the idea has to shape, enact the rhetoric. There is no concept, I feel, that can stand on its own with great clarity if the writing is workmanlike or clumsy. So to me the writing of the theory, the writing of the concept, is very very important. Quite often I sort of inspire myself by starting out—even my theoretical, conceptual pieces—by reading works that inspire me to a certain fineness of expression. One of the things I often do is to read some completely unconnected work before I start writing, most often poetry. For example, I often read W.H. Auden, who is a great favorite of mine, or I read Robert Lowell—just as a matter of practice, just as a sort of ritual to begin writing a piece, even though it has nothing to do with the piece.

So, I have a great respect and desire for fine writing. Often I will use a word that stretches a point just because I feel that it takes the thought somewhat further than it may need to go, but the suggestiveness of that word both enacts a kind of finer sense and sentiment, even though it would have been easier to close it down with a more workmanlike word that would have done the job and nailed it down. But I prefer to keep that open. I remember Toni Morrison saying to me once, "Writing is all." If you can't do it in the writing and through the writing, if you can't do this whole kind of revisionary history of slavery and sexuality that she's involved in in some of her work, if you can't do it in and through the actual writing, you can't do it by giving people ideas or thoughts. The two things really have to work together. That is what I try to do. In a way, writing to me is the staging of an idea, and I use that term with its full theatrical and operatic and dramatic possibilities, in the way in which the concept might be the armature or the architecture of the idea.

Q. Do you believe that writers and teachers of writing should problematize the dynamics of discourse by introducing discussions of sententiousness?

A. Yes, I think so. Sententiousness is a particular ideology of rhetoric, and it has a particular history. Eighteenth-century sententiousness, for instance, was a very dominant form. It was related to various discourses like the law or political edicts. It is part of a rhetoric of governance and authority. So, I think some awareness of what sententiousness is—as a production, as a process of communication, its conditions—is very important. I also think that it is very important to teach students, people, to write in a way that is clear, to communicate what it is that they want to say effectively so that they can feel represented. There is no totality of representation, but I think people should feel—in the sentence, if you will, in the language—that they can represent themselves. I know that this links to the question of literacy, which is a very important subject that we'll discuss later. However, like all pedagogical forms, I think sententiousness must also keep open for itself the possibility that the place where the sentence falls, where it will be taken up again, where the pause occurs in the sententiousness, where there is a hesitation within it, is not just a disturbance. It's not just an abnormality of the sententiousness, but it could be the place for resistance to its authority, for the reelaboration of its object of attention.

What's important to me is the possibility of seeing the borders of sententiousness as porous, not in some simple dyadic form in which sententiousness is the authoritative and nonsententiousness is the marginal or the subaltern or the resistance, not at all like this—but to continually see sententiousness as transforming. As Henry James once said, these are forms of relationship that really don't end anywhere; sententiousness is itself an emergence. Understanding that it is itself not an origin but an emergence is very important because then one is open to other residual and emergent and marginal forms of meaning-making or communication or subject identification. So I think my suggestion that we should look in a way beyond the sentence is not to say, as is often said now in a kind of flippant way, that we should move beyond rationalism or something of that kind, or rationality. Rather, it is to say that there are other logics of signification to which we should be open, and the sentence can sometimes sentence us, in the imprisoning sense, to the kind of prison house of a particular language form.

Q. Do you place any limits on the political effectivity of writing?

A. I certainly do believe that writing is a political form. By *writing*—if I might use that word—and *inscription,* I'm not only talking about printed writing or writing as we usually understand it. I'm talking about the possibility of making a determining mark on a surface. It may be a social surface; it may be a visual screen. I'm talking about writing in the widest sense: a kind of ordering of things or ordering of communication in one way in the context of a wider contingent structure. That's what I'm talking about. Certain forms of ritual could be inscribed in that way; certain modes of political organization could be inscribed in that way too. Having said that, let me say that I do feel that even in the more narrow sense writing is—and composition is—a highly political activity. It's a political activity. There is a politics of instruction, a politics of composition. Too often writing—in the broadest sense—is treated as a communicational medium where the subjects of that communication are constituted prior to the writing, where the objects of that communication are also constituted prior to that writing, and where the task of writing is seen as transparently mediating between already pregiven subjects, pregiven objects, and a preconstituted *mise en scène*. My interest is in suggesting that the agency of writing actually constitutes in a dialogic way new relationships between elements that may or may not be pregiven such that the pregivenness is questioned, the preconstitutedness is questioned. Of course, there are certain conditions, certain determinants that precede a particular act of communication, or writing, or mediation; but what happens in and through the writing is the reconjugation of those given conditions, and that is what I believe to be the effectivity of writing as a kind of agency, as a performance, as a practice, and as a process that is too little understood.

I have talked about metaphoricity because metaphoricity is one of those even more widely recognized moments when you have to stop and think where the writing act is going, what it is trying to constitute beyond what it is in some transparent way saying—the doubleness of the inscriptive act. So, I do think the activity of writing is, in that sense, a continually revisionary, and in some ways revolutionary, activity. I don't mean "revolutionary" with a capital *R*, not in some sort of political-adventurist sense, as I could be understood to mean. I'm just saying that it's a continual movement. In the "Minority Maneuvers and Unsettled Negotiations" essay in *Critical Inquiry*, it was my purpose to talk about political movement as movement, and indeed writing itself as a kind of movement.

I just want to add that we've talked about this active and even proactive—indeed, even revisionary—sense of writing. And I've tried to think, in the widest sense, of what politics might be conceived in that way. I just want to add that writing, therefore, is itself a mediation. It's not a medium; it's a mediation. Critics, philosophers, and political thinkers are so easily able to conceive of the mediatory nature of individuals, for instance, or of a particular kind of institutional form. But in a way, writing, which scribbles over all these things, subtends them—writing in the widest sense as the inscription of a mark, the making of an order—is somehow relegated to a transparency, as if it is following on from positions, objects, subjects already constituted. So it's this that I'm trying to get at.

Q. You write in *The Location of Culture*, "I have chosen to demonstrate the importance of the space of writing, and the problematic of address, at the very heart of the liberal tradition because it is here that the myth of the 'transparency' of the human agent and the reasonableness of political action is most forcefully asserted. . . . What the attention to rhetoric and writing reveals is the discursive ambivalence that makes 'the political' possible." This view suggests that the crucial function of the textual and the rhetorical is to make political struggle possible by drawing attention to discursive ambivalence.

A. Yes, I think that's a fair reading, but let's flesh it out. What address does is to draw your attention—if I may be figurative—not only to the place where the sign emerges in a particular discourse or a particular speech act, but how it flies and then falls at a point of relocation. That's what address is—how it moves from one space to another. Now, ambivalence is very important in order to contest forms of rationalism (not rationality but rationalism) that want to ascribe certain kinds of intentionality and achieved intentionality, as somehow flying through this transparent and immaterial medium. My emphasis on address is always to suggest that where the sign emerges and where it ends up may have incommensurable and contradictory terrains of inscription at either end. So to that extent, where address addresses the problem of the construction of social meaning or the ascription of a person or peoples, and so on, the important thing about writing and indeed the ambivalent structure of the sign in its emergence and its destination is to be aware that politically we are continually constructing the constituencies that we address, just as we are constructing the objects of value that we are transmitting. This, therefore, does not enable you to give a universal and transhistorical value to things like virtue or tolerance or secularism—or indeed the sacred. I think this makes you each time reinterrogate, because you are constructing the constituency and, indeed, the consistency of language and thought which you are then pointing to digitally.

Q. In "DissemiNation," you identifiy literacy as one of the instruments for narrating the nation. Would you elaborate on what you see as the role that literacy and literacy instruction— writing—play in the constitution and interrogation of the nation?

A. This is a very important question, and coming as I do from India, it has a very specific significance for me. I feel that literacy is connected intimately and institutionally with the question of democratic representation. It's more complex than saying that you can't really have a one-person one-vote system unless you have literacy because people are open then to all kinds of pressures, particularly in poorer countries where votes can be bought and sold. (Of course, votes can be bought and sold in Chicago or in any other place.) It's not limited to the South. But I do think that literacy is absolutely crucial for a kind of ability to be responsible to yourself, to make your own reading within a situation of political and cultural choice. In the Indian context, fascinatingly, the state of Kerala in the south has the highest literacy, that literacy fostered very much by Jesuit and other Catholic missionaries. And Kerala has been (or was until recently; I'm not sure of the situation at the moment) the state that had communist rule in an unbroken period of fifteen or twenty years. So there was a particular collaboration between Catholicism, communism, literacy, and democratic development.

Literacy is very important for the representation of "self," by which I don't mean individuals, just self-representation within a democratic foundation. But I think that there's no doubt that literacy is also in some ways an equalizing force. There is a danger of course in fetishizing literacy, the kind of fetishism when people say (and I'm talking about literacy in the more general sense), "We have this terrible racism, and it's because people don't know enough about another's culture. They don't know how to appreciate another's language or cuisine." That's a load of crap. Racism is often the leading ideology of the most educated and literate people. So, that's not important. But I think the kind of composition, the kind of writing, the kind of literacy that *we* have been talking about—which is not merely about competence but is about intervention, the possibility of interpretation as intervention, as interrogation, as relocation, as revision—is often not taught even at the best institutions and should be talked about and taught much more.

❦ ❦ ❦

Judith Butler

Q. Do you think consciously about the problems of writing as you are composing? Do you think of yourself as a writer?

A. I think that in general one thinks consciously about what one is composing but that what one is composing also happens in a way that exceeds one's own consciousness of what one does. So, for example, after I finish writing something I can look back and see that I have made implicit citations to other styles of writing without knowing that that's what I have done, or that I've tried to achieve something by pushing grammar in certain ways because what I was trying to think about couldn't quite be contained within the grammar that was available to me at the time. There's a *certain* level of consciousness to my writing process. I write and edit as I go along, and I'm not even sure one can, strictly speaking, distinguish between writing and editing. I know that people say that writing comes first and then editing comes later, but I think that's actually not true. It may actually be the reverse that's true: one edits in order to write.

I was trained in continental philosophy, and that meant that I spent a considerable amount of time reading Hegel and took numerous seminars on Heidegger; the difficulty of the language was in some ways essential to the philosophical views that were being expressed. For instance, when Hegel talks about the "speculative sentence," he is trying to work against the propositional form as it's been received. When he says, "The subject is spirit," the first inclination, the one that received grammar in some sense prepares us for, is to establish "the subject" as the subject of the sentence, and then "spirit" becomes one way of determining or qualifying that subject. But, of course, what he wants us to be able to do is to reverse that sentence, to recognize something about how the "is" functions: it doesn't just point linearly in one direction; rather, it points in both directions at once. He wants us to be able to experience the simultaneity of that sentence as it functions in its double directionality. Now, that's a very hard thing to do given how profoundly inclined we are by what Nietzsche called the "seductions of grammar" to read in a linear way. Reading Heidegger as a young person and trying to figure out what it is he was trying to do with his neologisms and his coinages also influenced me. Some people, such as Bourdieu, have dismissed it completely, but I think there was and remains a rather profound effort there to call into question ordinary language and the ways in which we structure the world on its basis, an analysis of the kinds of occlusions or concealments that take place when we take ordinary language to be a true indicator of reality as it is and as it must be.

So, submitting myself to what were profound grammatical challenges—challenges to grammar, challenges to ordinary language—was part of my own formation, and it was very exhilarating. I would even say that such texts were in a way the high modernism of the continental philosophical tradition, in that you have a similar experience as if you were to pick up the works of Mallarmé, or Celan, or even Proust: there are times when you think, "My God, what's happened to the sentence? Where's the sentence?" There's something in the life of the sentence that's become new or odd or estranging in some fundamental way—and I went for that. I was very much seduced by what I think was a high modernist notion that some newness of the world was going to be opened up through messing with grammar as it has been received. What concerns me is that this impulse—which I consider to be important to critical thinking and to an openness to what is new—has been disparaged by those who believe that we have a certain responsibility to write not only in an accessible way, but within the terms of already accepted grammar. What concerns me is that the critical relation to ordinary grammar has been lost in this call for radical accessibility. It's not that I'm in favor of difficulty for difficulty's sake; it's that I think there is a lot in ordinary language and in received grammar that constrains our thinking—indeed, about what a person is, what a subject is, what gender is, what sexuality is, what politics can be—and that I'm not sure we're going to be able to struggle effectively against those constraints or work within them in a productive way unless we see the ways in which grammar is both producing and constraining our sense of what the world is.

Q. In a recent piece in the *New York Times*, you explain the role of the contemporary tradition of critical theory, pointing out that "difficult language can change a tough world." You argue that language that challenges common sense can "help point the way to a more socially just world." Yet, many commentators, both within the academy and in the public sector, have taken aim at academic discourse in general, particularly that discourse (as you point out) that focuses on topics such as sexuality, race, nationalism, and the workings of capitalism. What do you believe is really at stake in these criticisms? Is this debate really about "good writing"?

A. No, I don't believe it's a debate about good writing. Sure, there is a problem when writing in the academy becomes so rarefied or so specialized that it speaks only to an in-crowd or to a group of people who are initiated into the protocols of the discourse. I've certainly seen that. There were times when deconstructive literary criticism became so internal to itself that unless you were trained in the exact same way and had read all the same texts and knew all the same allusions and understood all the same rhetorical gestures it was going to be a very odd and strange and alienating enterprise. I understand that. I believe it is important that intellectuals with a sense of social responsibility be able to shift registers and to work at various levels, to communicate what they're communicating in various ways. I think I probably do that, both in my writing and in my teaching, but it's always possible to seize upon the more specialized moments of my writing and to say that it is somehow exemplary—and that is unfair.

I'm interested in why there is an upsurge of anti-intellectualism in the academy right now. Is there guilt about being an intellectual? Is there guilt about being an intellectual because we don't know what effects, if any, the intellectual (especially the intellectual in the humanities) can have on the larger social world? There are some people on the left in the academy who believe that all you have to do is make certain verbal gestures and be publicly identified with certain kinds of verbal gestures in order to qualify as a politically minded intellectual. That is, you don't actually work in labor politics or give time to gay and lesbian activism or any of the rest; you simply identify publicly with certain stands. But even this is a haunted and guilty moment because the intellectual who believes that political satisfaction is to be gained through the public performance of certain kinds of verbal gestures is still not sure what effect that has. One gets to know in effect that one is being identified with certain positions, and so one gets *positioned*, you might say, within the academic landscape as a "leftist," as a "progressive," or as something else. Part of it is a structural problem in that people in the humanities no longer know whether they're central to the academy; they know that they're derided by the outside, and they don't know how to articulate how their work can have concrete effects on the lives of the students and the world in which they live. And there's a certain scapegoating occurring. Those intellectuals who speak in a rarefied way are being scapegoated, are being purged, are being denounced precisely because they represent a certain anxiety about everyone's effect—that is, what effect are *any* of us having, and what effect *can* we have? So, there might be an identification and a projection occurring: the persons who are being scapegoated probably remind the scapegoaters too much of their own dilemma.

It's unfortunate because I believe it has to be the case (certainly since Marx it *has* been the case) that becoming a critical intellectual involves working hard on difficult texts. Capitalism is itself a difficult text. From Marx through Adorno, we learned that capitalism is an extremely difficult text: it does not show itself as transparent; it gives itself in enigmatic ways; it calls for interpretive hermeneutic effort. There is no question about it. We think things are the way they must be because they've become naturalized. The life of the commodity structures our world in ways that we take for granted. And what was Marx's point? Precisely to make the taken-for-granted world seem spectral, strange. And how does that work? It only works by taking received opinion and received *doxa* and really working through it. It means undergoing something painful and difficult: an estrangement from what is most familiar. Adorno understood this. In *Minima Moralia* he talks about the painfulness of passing through difficult language but how it is absolutely essential to developing a critical attitude toward the constituted social world if we're not to take the constituted social world—that is to say the social world— as it is given, as it is rendered not only *familiar* but *natural* for us. That's a painful process, and not everybody wants to undergo it.

It may well be that we want to construct a fiction called "the public sphere," or a fiction called "common sense," or a fiction called "accessible meaning" that would allow us to think and feel for a moment as if we all inhabit the same linguistic world. What does it mean to dream of a common sense? What does it mean to want that today, at the beginning of the twenty-first century, when there's enormous conflict at the level of language? When Serbian and Croatian are now claiming they are separate languages? When speaking even in a Berkeley classroom means speaking across inflection, across dialect, across genres of academic writing to students for whom English is very often a second language? Every classroom I've ever been in is a hermeneutic problem. It's not as if there's a "common" language. I suppose if I were to speak in the language of the television commercial, I might get a kind of uniform recognition—at least for a brief moment—but I'm not going to be able to presuppose a common language in my classroom. I was teaching Rousseau's *Essay on the Origin of Languages* to a lecture course in modern rhetorical theory—it's a beautiful essay, very paradoxical, very complicated—and at one point Rousseau takes issue with the common conception of what onomatopoeia means. He says that you think that it is an instance in which the word we use in language approximates the sound that we hear in the world. So, for instance, the word *meow* actually sounds very much like the noise that the cat makes. We assume that language in some sense represents a pre-linguistic sound and that it is fully mimetic at that moment, that it's fully representative, that it's as close to a certain kind of mimetic proximity as one can get between language and thing. But, he says, it's not true. Cats say various things (or speak various ways or make various sounds) in various languages, and it's more the case that the word we have for the sound prepares us to hear the sound in a certain way. This is a very Wittgensteinian point, really—a pre- or proto-Wittgensteinian point.

So, I looked up at my classroom of eighty students and asked, "How many of you speak another language besides English?" Probably fifty-five of them raised their hands. And I asked, "Okay, what languages do you speak?" We went around the room, and there were probably sixteen languages represented in the class: Korean, Chinese, Japanese, Urdu, French, German, Spanish, Portuguese, and more. Then I asked, "What do cats say in your languages?" And we got sixteen *different* sounds, all of which claimed to be onomatopoetic. And the assumption in every single language was that *this* is what cats truly sound like. So the point was made, and it was fabulous. Cats say, "mah." Cats say, "mew." They say, "eee." Cats say lots of things. You have no idea what they say. Now, this was not just a lesson about how Rousseau was right; it was a lesson about multilingualism in the classroom. What does it mean to say that there is *a* language that is common, that everyone understands, and that it is somehow our social responsibility to speak? It seems to me that our social responsibility is to become attuned to the fact that there is *no* common language anymore. Or if there is a common language, it is the language of a commercialism that seeks to extend the hegemony of commercial American English, and to do it in a way that violently effaces the problem of multilingualism. This is one of the most profound pedagogical problems of our time, if not one of the most profound political problems of our time.

Q. You have written, "To call a presupposition into question is not the same as doing away with it; rather, it is to free it from its metaphysical lodgings in order to understand what political interests were secured in and by that metaphysical placing, and thereby to permit the term to occupy and to serve very different political aims." This statement seems to characterize your critical practice in general. Do you agree?

A. Yes, I do agree. That was an important thing to say. People are very much afraid of criticism; they think criticism is destructive. I wonder, though, whether it's not time to rethink what we mean by critique and the tradition of critique that was established really with Kant and that goes through critical theory and that emerges quite interestingly in Foucault (I think his short piece, "What Is Critique?" is generally under-read) and in Walter Benjamin when he writes about the critique of violence, for instance. That sense of critique has to be dissociated from a sense of destruction or pure negation. What it's really about is opening up the possibility of questioning what our assumptions are and somehow encouraging us to live in the anxiety of that questioning without closing it down too quickly. Of course, it's not for the sake of anxiety that one should do it (I don't think one should do anything for the sake of anxiety), but it's because anxiety accompanies something like the witnessing of new possibilities. It is important to call things into question. That does not mean one does away with them; it just means that one asks important questions: "What purposes have they served? What purposes can they serve? How can this term be mobilized beyond its established context to assume new meanings in new contexts?" The qualification I would add now, seven years later, is that although one can very often take a term like "masculine" and dislodge it from its metaphysical moorings—one can say, for example, that "masculine" does not necessarily apply exclusively to ostensibly anatomically male bodies and that it can function in another way, like, let's say, in the way that Judith Halberstam talks about "female masculinities"—it is important to question what of the prior context is brought forward as a kind of residue or trace. It is also important to question what new ontological effects the term can achieve, because to liberate it from its prior moorings in an established ontology is not to say that it will not acquire a new one.

Spivak understood this when she reneged on her notion of "strategic essentialism." She at first thought she'd be able to use a term like "Third-World woman" and just have it be strategic rather than metaphysically grounded. It didn't have to describe her (or anyone else) fully or exhaustively; it could be relieved of its descriptive function. But, of course, it *does* begin to describe, because the author who strategically intends it as *"X, Y,* or *Z"* has also to recognize that the semantic life of the term will exceed the intention of the strategist and that as it travels through discourse, it can take on new ontological meanings and become established in ways that one never intended. So, I guess I would be a little less optimistic about the possibility of a radical unmooring than I was in 1993.

Q. Many of your works are controversial, and so it is no surprise that some scholars would disagree with you. Nancy Fraser, for example, has voiced some criticisms of your work. Are there any misunderstandings or misrepresentations of your work that you would especially like to address at this time?

A. I'm always glad to have Nancy's arguments. I feel that we have a productive disagreement. I guess I'll say one thing about one of the points she regularly makes. Nancy and some other social theorists who are profoundly influenced by the Habermasian school worry that I am always interested in producing new possibilities but that I don't say which possibilities are good to pursue and which are bad to pursue, that I don't have a set of strong norms that would tell us which possibilities to actualize and which not. Certainly, I don't want *all* possibilities realized, so why don't I distinguish among them? What I would answer to that is that when we ask the question, "How ought we to live and what possibilities should we collectively seek to realize?" we always ask it within a given horizon of possibilities that are already established—what is imaginable. What worries me is that we very often make decisions about what life to pursue and what possibilities to realize without ever asking how our very notions of "what is possible," "what is livable," "what is imaginable" are constrained in advance, and maybe in some very politically consequential ways. For instance, say you're in a human rights organization that hasn't thought about the problem of gay and lesbian human rights—violence against gays and lesbians, the radical pathologization or psychiatrization or imprisonment of gays and lesbians. And say you are considering which strategies to pursue in the field but that the field of possibilities is delimited in advance such that gay and lesbian lives are not thinkable within the field. What does it mean to make a normative judgment on that basis when you have not critically interrogated *how* the field of possibility is itself constituted, and constituted through some pretty violent exclusions? It's not as if I wouldn't make such decisions or don't think there are hard decisions to make; what worries me is that the rush to *decision-ism* and to strong normativity very often fails to consider what is meant by some of the very basic terms that it assumes. For example, what is a deciding person? How are decisions made? What is the field of possibilities that is delimited in advance to me? What is outside that field? I worry that there is a critical dimension to political normativity (and even a normative dimension) that is missing, because if there's a violent circumscription of the possible—that is to say, certain lives are not considered lives, certain human capacities are not considered human—what does it mean that we take that for granted as we proceed to decide what we ought and ought not to do? It means that in our effort to be normative we perform a violence and an exclusion for which we are not accountable, and in my view that produces a massive contradiction.

Of course, Martha Nussbaum has also made a very strong attack on me, but I think it actually has nothing to do with my work. It doesn't strike me as an engaged or careful reading, and I presume that it does probably epitomize a certain frustration that a certain kind of liberal American politics has with a critical approach to some of its most important issues. She wants to be able to make strong paternalistic claims about women's conditions; she wants to be able to use the language of universality without interrogating it; she wants to be able to tell us how Indian women suffer; and she wants to be able to, in her words, make "an assault" on local cultures when it is mandated by universal concerns. I see her as being very much opposed to the problem of cultural translation and cultural difference; she thinks they get in the way of strong normative arguments. We can see something like a resurgence of a certain kind of white feminism here that doesn't want to have to hear about difference, that wants to be able to make its strong claims and speak in the name of "reason," and speak in the name of *everyone* without having to hear them, without having to learn what it might mean to hear them. So, I'm sorry about that. It seems to me to be full of a kind of displaced animosity, but I think people can read it for what it is.

Let me make one final comment. You've asked me about difficult writing, and you've asked me whether I think the State has any role in the adjudication of hate speech. These are in effect questions about whether what I write is readable, whether what I am for is translatable into contemporary politics in an obvious or clear way. I think that I probably produce a certain amount of anxiety, or what Foucault calls the politics of discomfort, and I don't do that just to be annoying. For me, there's more hope in the world when we can question what is taken for granted, especially about what it is to be a human, which is a really fundamental question. What qualifies as a human, as a human subject, as human speech, as human desire? How do we circumscribe human speech or desire? At what cost? And at what cost to whom? These are questions that I think are important and that function within everyday grammar, everyday language, as taken-for-granted notions. We feel that we know the answers. We know what family is, we know what desire is, we know what a human subject is, we know what speech is, we know what is comprehensible, we know its limits. And I think that this feeling of certainty leads to a terrible parochialism. Taking for granted one's own linguistic horizon as the ultimate linguistic horizon leads to an enormous parochialism and keeps us from being open to radical difference and from undergoing the discomfort and the anxiety of realizing that the scheme of intelligibility on which we rely fundamentally is not adequate, is not common, and closes us off from the possibility of understanding others and ourselves in a more fundamentally capacious way.

❦ ❦ ❦

Noam Chomsky

Q. Do you think of yourself as a writer?

A. I've never particularly thought of myself as a writer. In fact, most of what I've published are written-up versions of lectures. For example, *Syntactic Structures*, the first book that actually appeared, was essentially lecture notes for an undergraduate course at MIT, revised slightly to turn them into publishable form. I would say probably eighty or ninety percent of the work I do on political issues is sort of working out notes from talks. Much of the material that ends up as professional books is based on class lectures or lectures elsewhere, so I tend to think out loud.

The fact is that most of the writing I do is probably letters. I spend about twenty hours a week, I guess, just answering letters. Many of the letters are on questions that are in response to the hundreds of letters that I receive which are thoughtful and interesting and raise important questions (here's today's batch). Hundreds go out every week, and that requires thought; some of them are rather long. Those are actually written without being spoken. Sometimes I do sit down and write a book, too, but most of the time I don't think of myself as a writer particularly.

Q. You *have* had a few words to say about your writing process: "I'm able to work in twenty-minute spurts. I can turn my attention from one topic to another without start-up time. I almost never work from an outline or follow a plan. The books simply grow by accretion."

A. The reason for the twenty-minute spurts—which is a bit of an exaggeration; maybe hour spurts would be more accurate—is just the nature of my life, which happens to be very intense. I have two full-time professional careers, each of them quite demanding, plus lots of other things. I just mentioned one—lots and lots of correspondence—and other things as well, and that doesn't leave much time. In fact, my time tends to be very chopped up. I discovered over the years that probably my only talent is this odd talent that I seem to have that other colleagues don't, and that is that I've got sort of buffers in the brain that allow me to shift back and forth from one project to the other and store one. I can pick up after a long stretch and be more or less where I left off. In fact, I've sometimes had to. I have friends like this. I had, in particular, one friend who just died a couple of years ago who was an Israeli logician and who'd been an old friend since I was twenty or so. We would meet every five or six years and usually pick up the conversation we had been having as if we had just had it five minutes ago and go on from there.

As far as my books just sort of writing themselves, that's pretty much what happens. I don't recall ever having sat down and planned a book—except maybe for saying, "Well, I'm going to talk about X, Y, and Z, and I'll have Chapter One on X, Chapter Two on Y, and Chapter Three on Z." Then it's just a matter of getting the first paragraph, and it just goes on from there. It's probably because I've thought about most of it before, or lectured on it before, or written a letter to someone about it, or done it twenty times in the past. Then it becomes mainly a problem of trying to fit it all in. I *have* discovered, if it's of any interest to you, that I write somewhat differently now that I have a computer— quite a bit differently. I don't know if it shows up any different, but I know I write differently. I was very resistant to the computer. I didn't want to use it, and finally the head of the department just stuck it in my room. My teenage son who was—like every teenager, I guess—a super hacker carried me gently through the early stages, which I never would have had the patience to do. Once I was able to use the computer, I discovered that there were a lot of things that I could do that I'd never done before. For example, I'd never done much editing, simply because it was too much trouble; I didn't want to retype everything. And I never did much in the way of inserting and rearranging and so on. Now

I do a fair amount of that because it's so easy. Whether that shows up differently for the reader, I don't know. But I know I'm writing quite differently.

Q. For you, what are the most important elements of rhetoric?

A. I don't have any theory of rhetoric, but what I have in the back of my mind is that one should not try to persuade; rather, you should try to lay out the territory as best you can so that other people can use their own intellectual powers to work out for themselves what they think is right or wrong. For example, I try, particularly in political writing, to make it extremely clear in advance exactly where I stand. In my view, the idea of neutral objectivity is largely fraudulent. It's not that I take the realistic view with regard to fact, but the fact is that everyone approaches complex and controversial questions—especially those of human significance—with an ax to grind, and I like that ax to be apparent right up front so that people can compensate for it. But to the extent that I can monitor my own rhetorical activities, which is probably not a lot, I try to refrain from efforts to bring people to reach my conclusions.

It's just kind of an authoritarian practice one should keep away from. The same is true for teaching. It seems to me that the best teacher would be the one who allows students to find their way through complex material as you lay out the terrain. Of course, you can't avoid guiding because you're doing it a particular way and not some other way. But it seems to me that a cautionary flag should go up if you're doing it too much because the purpose is to enable students to be able to figure out things for themselves, not to know this thing or to understand that thing but to understand the next thing that's going to come along; that means you've got to develop the skills to be able to critically analyze and inquire and be creative. This doesn't come from persuasion or forcing things on people. There's sort of a classical version of this—that teaching is not a matter of pouring water into a vessel but of helping a flower to grow in its own way—and I think that's right. It seems to me that that's the model we ought to approach as best possible. So I think the best rhetoric is the least rhetoric.

Q. You've emphasized that there is this strong element of innateness in language. What about written language?

A. I'm sure if we look at written language we're going to find the conditions of Plato's problem arising once again. Namely, we just know too much. The basic problem that you always face when you look at human competence, or for that matter at any biological system, is that the state it has attained is so rich and specific that you cannot account for it on the basis of interactions, such as learning, for example. That's something that's found almost universally. The case of puberty is only one example, but it's true from the level of the cell on up. When you look at any form of human activity, whether it's speech or moral judgment or ability to read, I think you'll find exactly the same thing. When you understand the actual phenomenon, what you discover typically is that there's some kind of triggering effect from the outside— often what we call "teaching" or "learning"—that sets in motion inner directive processes. That's how you can gain such rich competence on the basis of such limited experience. It's not unlike the fact that when a child eats, it grows. The food makes it grow, if you like, but it's not the food that's determining the way it grows; the way it grows is determined by its inner nature. It won't do it without food; if you keep the food away, the child won't grow. But when you give the child the food, it's going to grow into what it's going to be, a human and not a bird, and the reason for that is the inner nature. That's basically Plato's argument.

Q. Paulo Freire and others argue that writing, because it can lead to "critical consciousness," is an avenue to social and political empowerment of the disenfranchised. Do you agree?

A. Absolutely. In fact, writing is an indispensable method for interpersonal communication in a complicated society. Not in a hunter-gatherer tribe of fifteen people; then you can all talk to one another. But in a world that's more complicated than that, intellectual progress and cultural progress and moral progress for that matter require forms of interaction and communicative interchange that go well beyond that of speaking situations. So, sure, people who can participate in that have ways of enriching their own thought, of enlightening others, of entering into constructive discourse with others which they all gain by. That's a form of empowerment. It's not the case if a teacher tells the kid, "Write five-hundred words saying this." That's just a form of reducing; that's a form of de-education, not education. Doing things that will stimulate critical analysis, self-analysis, and analysis of culture and society is very crucial. In fact, it seems to me that part of the core of all education ought to be the development of systems of intellectual self-defense and also stimulation of the capacity for inquiry, which means also collective inquiry. And this is one of the domains in which it can be done. It is done, say, in the natural sciences, but localized in those problems. It ought to be done in a way so that people understand that this is a general need and a general capacity; English composition courses are perfectly appropriate places for that.

Donald Davidson

Q. How would you describe your writing style?

A. A friend of mine, Arnold Isenberg, once told me—I think before I had written anything—that the way to write a paper in philosophy was to begin by asking a question that anybody could understand or by posing a problem in such a way that anyone would see that it was a problem. I followed that advice for a long time and began most of my papers with either a problem or a question, so I have attempted always to write my essays in such a way that the reader does not require any special background in philosophy in order to understand my meaning. I'm often told that my papers are difficult, but that was certainly never my aim. My aim was quite in the other direction. I'm gratified by the fact that people who don't have any technical background in philosophy do seem to make something of my ideas. I think the only other thing I can say about my style is that I sometimes find it incredibly hard to start writing. I often imagine the first sentence and then ask myself, "Wait! What comes next?" Pretty soon, I'm writing the whole paper in my head, and any problem in the composition or organization of the text stops me from even writing the first sentence for fear I would be somehow trapped. When I do finally write something, I often find that the first couple of pages, which usually sort of ease me into the subject, are better left out. So, I'll throw away these painfully constructed early pages completely.

I don't do a great deal of revising. I always believe that I have a pretty clear idea about how a paper is going to go together before I start writing. However, in the throes of composing a paper, I find that I regularly think about the paper. When I'm trying to go to sleep or when I'm half asleep, ways of putting things often occur to me, or when I'm not in the midst of writing, a new idea or a solution for some problem of organization sometimes will come to me. I find that these relaxed moments—when I am not actually writing—are absolutely essential in my composing process.

I don't think I've ever had any substantial help from an editor. I've often wished I had. The kind of thing I usually get from editors is advice on how to punctuate. For example, I've had several battles with the *Journal of Philosophy*. Concerning the first piece of mine that they published, the editors insisted that periods and commas go inside quotation marks and semi-colons and colons go outside. They said that this method of punctuation is absolutely standard practice in the United States. I wrote back and said, "Not so: the *New Yorker* does it the way I do it." Whereupon, they backed down. Aside from the fixation that the editor of the *Journal of Philosophy* had about punctuation and "whiches" and "thats," I can't remember much guidance from an editor. I should point out, however, that I often circulate a paper to colleagues and friends and ask them to make suggestions or comments, but they never do. The suggestions usually come years later after the paper has been published. Where I do receive a lot of help is from reading my papers aloud to audiences. In these presentations, I almost always get good ideas about what is difficult, what could be phrased in a better way, and so forth. Such feedback is extremely valuable because I see what it is that troubles people, and I realize there are difficulties I hadn't noticed. . . .

At the beginning of our discussion, you touched on the topic of writing, and it's something that I have some thoughts about. I do think there is a big difference between communication by writing and by speech. In what I think of as the best kind of teaching, this difference comes very much to the fore. As it seems to me, words which are extremely important to us—especially the big words that philosophers are fond of like truth, good, right, courage, sincerity—really do change in force according to the situation in which they're used. There are cases where we're apt to agree whether these words apply or don't, and then there's a huge shadowy area which often concerns cases that don't come up all the time or even cases that we just imagine for the sake of exploring the concepts. In the course of talking, we temporarily sharpen concepts through dialogue. That can't happen in writing, at least in the same way. So, I think that in conversation itself, we give words shapes, especially these big words which are important but vague. Perhaps these shapes will be ones that will remain with us after the discussion. A whole lot of philosophy is like that and teaching, too, if it's done right. It's a matter of people discovering what they think. It's not a matter of people bringing sharp ideas into conflict and then deciding who's right. That can happen, too, but much more important is the situation in which ideas are taking shape as the conversation goes on.

Q. How does writing fit with your metaphor of "triangulation"?

A. First of all, it seems to me that a lot of different cases exist. If you have two people who are dumb sitting next to each other and writing notes, then the fact that the note is written hardly makes any difference. It's the same thing as talking. If they're writing each other letters, well now a difference has occurred. For example, certain kinds of indexical gestures are lost. You can't point to something in a letter. Temporal references slip and so on. If you're writing a proclamation to a group, then further indexical elements drop out, because you're not sharing your ideas just with one person but with a lot of them. If you're writing a will, you're not going to be there to interpret it. So, I envision a whole continuum. A novel, for example, is an especially interesting case, because typically the author does not expect interaction with the readers. It doesn't mean that there is no feedback; it's just not relevant in any very important way, unless you happen to be Rushdie. This lack of interaction surely does make a big difference with the triangulation idea, and you have to ask how to apply the idea. I think the only way to do this is to say that something like novel writing absolutely depends upon the prior existence of conversational exchange. People have to have been in the triangular situation before they could make anything out of a novel.

The normal way in which language gets related to the world is mostly lacking in a novel, or, let's say, it's deferred. It's established through indirect connections rather than direct ones. You can't learn what the proper names refer to from reading the book itself, and, of course, in a novel they normally don't refer to anything. You have to have learned it in some other situation. If someone were to talk about Paris and London or something like that, you can't learn from the book where they are, because the book can't point. The causal connections are lost to you; there's a lot of dependence upon the kind of case that I think of as basic. So, what is radical interpretation like when it comes to interpreting a book? I think that's a very tricky question and to tell you the truth, reading the essays in Reed Way Dasenbrock's volume

[*Literary Theory after Davidson*] has made me think about this. I'm surprised I didn't think of it before, since I began with a great interest in literature. I see that it's an extremely interesting question, and with all the discussion nowadays about the relevance of intention in interpretation, I need to think about some things I haven't thought about very hard. On the other hand, reading various things has made me realize that people who are talking about literary criticism need to make a lot of distinctions that they haven't been bothering about, at least the critics that I've been reading. They say either that intention matters or that it doesn't. Well, you really can't put it that way, because certain intentions on the part of the author must be known or assumed in order to make anything of the text at all. This is so outrageous an example that it may sound silly, but if we were to discover that the *Iliad* isn't in ancient Greek, that it's in an unknown language we just now learned to decipher and it doesn't mean anything of the sort that we thought it meant, would we go on reading it as being Greek? Some people say, "Yeah, read it any old way you please," but that seems wild. If we want to understand what's there, we need to know what the language is more or less. So, the intentions can't be totally irrelevant. There's no way that a book can say on its cover "understand this book as being in ancient Greek," because those very words may mean something else in the language it's written in.

Jacques Derrida

Q. Do you think of yourself as a writer?

A. It's difficult to answer this question without some preliminary precautions. I don't think of myself as a writer if by "writer" you mean merely a literary writer, an author of poems and fiction in the traditional sense. From that point of view, I'm not a writer. But neither am I a philosopher who writes or a theoretician who writes without being attentive to writing—to the form, techniques, and so on. So, I think of myself neither as a writer (in the sense of working within literary genres) nor as a scientist or philosopher who wouldn't be interested in questions of writing. I'm interested in the way I write, in the form, the language, the idiom, the composition. When I write a text—and I write different kinds of texts—I'm as attentive to, let's say, the content as to the formal style and also to the performative shape, the genre, all the aspects that belong to a given genre. All those problems which are traditionally called "formal" are what interest me most. To that extent, I think of myself as a sort of writer. But I'm unhappy with the boundaries between, let's say, literary writing and philosophical writing. I'm not a writer, but writing to me is the essential performance or act. I am unable to dissociate thinking, teaching, and writing. That's why I had to try to transform and to extend the concept of writing, which is not simply "writing down" something. So, "yes and no" would be the answer.

Q. Who were key "writing teachers" for you—not necessarily people who held official faculty positions, but people who advised you well about your writing or whose writing inspired your own composition processes?

A. There are a number of possible answers to this. Paradoxically, I learned a lot from my teachers both in high school and in what we call the *khâgne*—a grade between high school and the *Ecole Normale Supérieure*—the university. We had to prepare a composition we call the *concours d'entrée*. This instruction was very hard and heavy, very demanding according to classical norms. I was trained in those very classical norms. And probably people who read me and think I'm playing with or transgressing norms—which I do, of course—usually don't know what I know: that all of this has not only been made possible by but is constantly in contact with very classical, rigorous, demanding discipline in writing, in "demonstrating," in rhetoric. Even if I feel, or some of my readers think, that I am free or provocative toward those norms, the fact that I've been trained in and that I am at some level true to this classical teaching is essential. I think that perhaps my American readers—when they read me in English, for example— don't or can't pay attention to the fact that this classical superego is very strong in terms of rhetoric, whether it's a question of rhetoric in the sense of the art of persuasion or in the sense of logical demonstration. When I take liberties, it's always by measuring the distance from the standards I know or that I've been rigorously trained in. So, my classical training in France has been a great influence—all those competitions that I suffered from. The French system was and still is terrible from that point of view; you have to go through a number of selective competitions which make you suffer to make you better. I'm politically against this system and I fight it; nevertheless, I had to go through it. Yet, however negative it may be from some point of view, it's good discipline and I learned a lot from it. The way I write is probably marked by this experience. So, first, there are those teachers at school. But then, you learn from everything you read; every writer or philosopher you admire is a kind of writing teacher. So I learned from many, many writers

Q. Anyone in particular?

A. No, because it depends on the type of text I write. I write different types of texts. I won't say I imitate—that's certainly not true—but I try to match in my own idiom the style or the way of writing of the writers I write on. When I write on Mallarmé, I don't write the same as when I write on Blanchot or Ponge. It's not a mimetic behavior, but I try to produce my own signature in relation to the signature of the other, so I don't learn a model way of writing. It's not learning; it's listening to the other and trying to produce your own style in proportion to the other. It's not a lesson you learn; it's something else.

Q. Would you describe this as being "influenced" by these authors?

A. It's not an "influence." Even though I write differently when I write on Mallarmé or Blanchot or Ponge, this difference doesn't mean that I'm under their influence. But I adjust. I don't write like Blanchot, but my tone changes; everything is differently staged, but I wouldn't speak of "influence." It's responding—responding to the other. Blanchot remains other, and I don't write the way he writes so my writing is other too. But this otherness is responding or co-responding, so to speak.

Q. Is writing, composition, taught in French universities?

A. No, there is no such instruction in France. We don't teach composition, as such. Of course, through the teaching of French and literature, there has been, or there should be, the concurrent teaching of composition. The teacher of French literature, for example, requires students to write correctly, elegantly, and so forth. There are grammatical and stylistic norms. But this is a very mobile situation. Now we are seeing problems that look or sound like yours. I wouldn't call it "illiteracy," but there has been a massive change during the last two decades. The level of what is required seems to have dropped, and this is something that everyone in my generation complains about. But it's not that simple, and I don't share these complaints. It is true that our norms are not respected, and we cannot recognize in children and young people now the same respect we had for spelling, and so on. In France the pedagogy which was built through the ideology of the Third Republic was very rigorous, and the social authority of the teacher was enormous. This meant that there was an ethics of spelling, of *orthographe*, and every transgression, every misspelling, was a crime. This was the case in my generation and before me. Now, of course, this is no longer the case, and respect for these values has disappeared, for the students and for the young teachers, too. But this doesn't mean that these people have given up any respect for anything; it's that the norms have changed. They're not less intelligent but their intelligence is applied differently, and it's very difficult for people from my generation to understand this shifting, this restructuring of the norms. So there is no teaching of composition, as such. There should be parallel teaching of composition everywhere: in the teaching of French literature, of history, and so on. Now, everyone believes that French young people, however intelligent they may be, don't read and write the way they should. This is the cause of much current anxiety in France. . . .

The word *composition*, as you know, is an old word, implying that you can distinguish between the meaning, the contents of the meaning, and the way you put these together. As you know, *deconstruction* means, among other things, the questioning of what synthesis is, what thesis is, what a position is, what composition is, not only in terms of rhetoric, but what *position* is, what *positing* means. Deconstruction questions the *thesis*, the theme, the positionality of everything, including, among other things, *composition*. Writing is not simply a "composition." So once you realize that writing is not simply a way of positing or posing things together, a number of consequences follow.

Without remaining at this level, which is radical—but we have to mention this radicality—I would say that in the university, or in high school, or in any academic field, deconstruction should provoke not only a questioning of the authority of some models in composition, but also a new way of writing, of composing—composing oral speeches and composing written papers. Now, this new way is not simply a new model; deconstruction doesn't provide a new model. But once you have analyzed and questioned and destabilized the authority of the old models, you have to invent each time new forms according to the situation, the pragmatic conditions of the situation, the audience, your own purpose, your own motivation to invent new forms. And these depend on what I call the "pragmatic" in the sense of speech act theory. In each situation you have to write and speak differently. Teachers should not impose a rigid scheme in any situation.

A moment ago, I was speaking of my training in France; the rigidity of those forms, those norms for rhetoric and composition, was terrible. It had some good aspects too, but it was terrible. You had to write what we called a *dissertation* according to certain pattern: in the introduction you should ask a question after having played naive; that is, you should act as if you do not know what the question is, then you *invent* the question, you justify the question, and at the end of the introduction you ask the question. Then in three parts you. . . . Well there's no need to describe the formula, but it was terribly rigid. So I think through deconstruction you should study and analyze these models and where they come from, where their authority comes from, what the finality of these models is, what interests they serve—personal, political, ideological, and so on. So we have to study the models and the history of the models and then try not to subvert them for the sake of destroying them but to change the models and invent new ways of writing—not as a formal challenge, but for ethical, political reasons. . . .

I'd like to make a point about rhetoric becoming the central paradigmatic, epistemic activity. On the one hand, I would think that we should not neglect the importance of rhetoric, as if it were simply a formal superstructure or technique exterior to the essential activity. Rhetoric is something decisive in society. On the other hand, I would be very suspicious of what I would call "rhetoricism"—a way of giving rhetoric all the power, thinking that everything depends on rhetoric as simply a technique of speech. Certainly, there are no politics, there is no society without rhetoric, without the force of rhetoric. Not only in economics but also in literary strategy, rhetoric is essential. Even among diplomats, rhetoric is very important; in the nuclear age much depends on some kind of rhetoric. (I tried to show this in an article called "No Apocalypse, Not Now" in *Diacritics*.) Now, this doesn't mean that everything depends on verbal statements or formal technique of speech acts. There are speech acts everywhere, but the possibility of speech acts, or performative speech acts, depends on conditions and conventions which are not simply verbal. What I call "writing" or "text" is not simply verbal. That's why I'm very interested in rhetoric but very suspicious of rhetoricism. . . .

I'm interested in the rhetoric hidden in philosophy itself because within, let's say, the typical Platonic discourse there is a rhetoric—a rhetoric against rhetoric, against sophists. I've been interested in the way concepts or arguments depend intrinsically on metaphors, tropes, and are in themselves to some extent metaphors or tropes. I'm not saying that all concepts are essentially metaphors and therefore everything is rhetoric. No, I try to deconstruct the opposition between concept and metaphor and to rebuild, to restructure this field. I'm not at ease with metaphor either. I'm not saying, "Well, we should just substitute metaphor for concept or simply be content with metaphors." What I say, for example, in *White Mythology* is that the concept of metaphor, first, is a metaphor; it's loaded with philosophy—a very old philosophy—and so we shouldn't keep the concept of metaphor the way it is commonly received. So I would distrust, suspect, the couple concept and metaphor. And I would, for the same reasons, be suspicious of the opposition between philosophy and rhetoric. To the extent that I am caught up within this couple, I'm a philosopher, but I try not to remain within this opposition. I try to understand what has happened since Plato and in a recurrent way until now in this opposition between philosophy and rhetoric. . . .

When sometimes I've used the word *rhetoricism*, it was not simply in reference to rhetoric. I remember having used this word as an accusation. I was not referring to what we call "rhetoric" or to the attention given to rhetoric. On the contrary, I am in favor of the most rigorous and most generous attention given to rhetoric.

What I'm suspicious of under the name "rhetoricism" is the authority of language. *Rhetoric* comes from, as you know, a Greek word meaning *speaking*. So, the charge of logocentrism or phonocentrism is, by itself, a charge against rhetoricism—not the narrow field of what we call rhetoric, but simply the authority of speech, the authority of speaking. If you give absolute privilege to rhetoric, you fall into what I call logocentrism or phonocentrism; that's what I meant when I spoke of rhetoricism. I was not charging anyone with being too attentive to rhetoric. I think we should be attentive to rhetoric and to language as much as possible, but the hegemony of speaking over anything else— writing, acting, and so on—is a kind of rhetoricism. So for me, rhetoricism in that context is synonymous with logocentrism or phonocentrism.

Q. Hélène Cixous and other French feminists advocate that women create a "women's language"—a language that inscribes femininity, a "new insurgent" language that liberates, ruptures, and transforms "phallogocentric" discourse. Are such strategies compatible with deconstruction, or do they merely replace one hierarchy with another?

A. Sometimes it does; it depends on the way women and sometimes men practice this writing, teaching, speaking, and so on. Sometimes feminism replaces phallogocentrism with another kind of hegemony. I wouldn't say that all women do that, but it's a structural temptation. It's perhaps inevitable at some point that they try to reverse the given hierarchy, but if they do only that— reverse the hierarchy—they would reinscribe the same scheme. Sometimes feminism, as such, does that, and I know that some women are not happy about that. You are quoting Hélène Cixous, a very old friend of mine whom I admire deeply, and she is, I would say, one of the greatest writers in France today. She, at some point, of course, spoke of "feminine writing," but I don't think she would still do that, if by "feminine writing" you refer to a specific essentially feminine way of writing. At some points in history, women have had to claim that there is some irreducible feminine way of writing—themes, style, position in the field of literature—not in order to essentialize this, but as a phase in the ongoing war or process or struggle. But if some of them—and I don't think this is the case with Hélène Cixous—would try to say it's the eternal essential feminine which is manifested in this feminine writing, then they would repeat the scheme they claim they are fighting.

❦ ❦ ❦

Michael Eric Dyson

Q. You are a prolific writer. How do you think of writing in the larger scope of black narrative?

A. Writing has become extraordinarily important in terms of black storytelling and in shaping and influencing black cultural expression, especially because of the centrality of narrative. The narrativity of black experience—the ways in which stories shape self-understanding and mediate self-revelation racially—is enormously powerful in narrative forms, especially autobiographical narratives, which constitute the attempt of the race both to state and then to move forward to its goals as revealed in stories of "overcoming odds," "up from slavery," and "out of the ghetto." Narrativity is an extraordinarily important component of self-understanding and the way in which African-American peoples constitute their own identities, especially in this postmodern world. Writing *per se*—the capacity of people to reflect critically upon their experiences and then filter those experiences through the lens of their own written work—certainly shapes and changes self-expression in a way different from, say, oral expression. In other words, as Ali Masri, the Africanist, says, there is something extraordinarily conservative about the oral form because it only preserves that which people remember and deem necessary to integrate into the fabric of their collective memory, whereas the written form contests certain narrow limitations of the oral form because it situates the writer and the reader in a trans-historical moment that allows the articulation of an extraordinary convergence of contested identities and conflicting identities. For instance, when we're writing and we have a body of writing to appeal to and a body of writing against which we can contrast our own self-understanding—our own self-revelation and self-invention against what Foucault said, against what Ellison said, against what Baldwin said, against what slave narratives have been talking about for the last century and as we've recuperated them—it is an extraordinarily different moment because the narrative community there constitutes a wedge of interpretation that is provided by the writing, the very physical act of having the paper to refer to.

In regard to the creation of the self through narrative, it is much different when you have an oral community where people are relying upon memory, upon the texture of their memory, to mediate their own self-understanding. Orality provides a different lens than writing does; writing is textured, embodied—what Haraway calls *material density*. The physical reality of the writing itself has a kind of phenomenological and epistemological *weight* levied against this memory because you can refer *to* the text, whereas in the oral traditions, they certainly have a kind of genealogical effect: one passes one thing on from another (as opposed to a kind of Nietzschian or Foucauldian sense of genealogy). The oral reference provides a kind of artifice of invented memory that in one sense is *not* the same as in written work.

So I think that writing is very important, and it's very important in terms of the transition of African peoples from modernist to postmodernist forms. Writing is enormously important to try to figure out what the past is about, what the present is about in relationship to that past, and how writing itself becomes a bridge of communication and connection between previous cultures and contemporary ones—*and* a way of reinventing the very character and texture of experience in light of one's own writing. Writing is as much about revelation as it's about invention. When one is writing, one is literally *writing into* and *writing from*, and those poles of writing into and writing from—inscribing and re-inscribing—situate the writer in a kind of interpretive and performative moment that allows the writer to be the mediator, to mediate between these two poles of invention. Especially for African-American people who are preoccupied with literacy, who are preoccupied with the articulation of a self through narrative, writing becomes a most important avenue of both revealing and inventing the future of the race.

Writing becomes, in relationship to other narrative forms, a crucial aspect of connecting ourselves to an old debate about black intelligence, but it also becomes a way of unleashing and constituting different forms of self-understanding that are necessary if we're to move beyond the *mere* fixation on the oral and the *mere* fixation on the cinematic to talk about the legitimate concern of literate expression. Black people have been torn in two directions here. On the one hand, we've said, "That's about white folk and what they do; that's about mainstream society and culture; black folks' abilities to articulate self-identity and revelation and culture are about orality, so writing is not a central part of our project." On the other hand, others have said, "No, *only* when we begin to write with a certain level of mastery and with those narrative patriarchal codes in place will we be able to exemplify our own specific form of mastery and intelligence, and then we will be in one sense entering the modern world and able to, in a very powerful way, show that we are worthy of participation in this American project of democracy and that we're worthy bearers of culture." What's important to me is not to discard writing as a central project of African and African-American peoples. There have been all kinds of writings embedded in black culture from the get-go. One of the things we have to see is that it's a deeply racist moment to suggest that writing (as opposed to orality) is about a tradition external to African-American culture. I see myself as a writer first and foremost in that sense: an articulator of speech, an articulator of ideas and the way in which ideas are not only mediated through speech but constituted in very powerful ways through the very act of writing, the physical weight of writing, the intellectual and ontological self-revelation that is expressed in writing.

We then have to figure out a way to link writing to a very powerful articulation of black culture, and this is where, for me, questions of authenticity come in. It's not "authentic" for black folk to write at a certain level; it's authentic for them to speak. It's not authentic for them to engage in intellectual performances; it's about the articulation of the self through the body. So all of these other narrative forms (cinema and forms of musical culture) have precedence in African-American culture because, as Hortense Spillers points out, these are the forms that were demanded during slavery. Slave masters didn't say, "Come and perform a trope for us; come and perform a metaphoric allegory." They said, "Come and perform a song for us, and come engage in physical activity." We have to refocus activity on black intellectual expression through narrative forms that become a way for black people to extend and investigate a tradition that we have neglected. The best of black cultural and literary scholars have begun to force us to rethink these issues in light of notions of multiple literacies and of the way in which most literacies are connected to certain forms of cultural expression within black society.

So, writing is central. As we move into this hypertext and cyberworld, and the way in which the forms of expression are mediated not through people's physical writing but through exchange via information systems, the recovery of writing becomes a kind of nostalgic project (already ironically at the end of the twentieth century) and also an articulation of the necessity of still having a mediating agent—that is, the *writer* not only standing in for a larger narrative community, but intervening with his or her own viewpoints about what constitutes authentic legitimate powerful black identity.

Q. How does language affect your own coming to terms with race?

A. That's a very powerful question. There's an old Bible passage, somewhere in the Psalms: "I was conceived in sin and born in iniquity." I feel that I was born in language; I feel that there's a verbal womb, a rhetorical womb, that I was nurtured in. My mother, who was a highly intelligent black woman, appreciated literacy but was prevented from it because she was a female and the youngest of a family of five children born to a farmer in Alabama. From the very beginning, I was bathed in the ethos of linguistic appreciation. My mother talked to us and read to us. And then I went to church; the church is a very important narrative community for me, very powerful—not only in terms of the norms it mediates in regard to the stances one should take politically and spiritually, but simply because of the resplendent resonances that were there in terms of language: hearing the power of articulations of black preachers, hearing the linguistic innovations of black singers, hearing the rhetorical dexterity of a revivalist who came to town to try to paint the picture of God dying on a cross and the differences that death made, not simply telling us about a theology of atonement, not simply talking to us (in dry, arcane, academized, theological language) about the dispensation of God. They wanted to paint a picture; they wanted us to feel it, to feel the kind of existential and ontological density of linguistic specificity. What I mean by "linguistic specificity" is that the language itself had a performative capacity, "performative" in the most enlarging and very powerful sense of that word. They not only were performing The Word from God, but they themselves, the words, were performing a kind of oracular and wisdom-tradition intervention upon our lives. That was extraordinarily important to me because I got a sense of the rhythms, the passions, the almost physical texture of language; I felt the very visceral dimensions of verbal articulation.

In elementary school, my fifth-grade teacher, Mrs. James (about whom I've written), had an extraordinary capacity to make black history come alive off the page, and she did so through teaching us painting and poetry. The poetry, especially, and writing our own stories was very important. Mrs. James encouraged us to see a direct connection between the capacities for invention and self-revelation from prior black generations and our own. She made the capacity to be a linguistic animal a very real and appealing one for us. She taught us that if we're really going to be powerful black people, intelligent black people, then we've got to do what other powerful, intelligent black people did: they wrote, they thought, they created.

As you say, I try to integrate a variety of perspectives about language in my own work now because I think that we should take note of what Derrida does with language and how he challenges straightforward traditional literary conceptions of language such as logocentrism. We've got to demythologize that through a kind of deconstructive practice that asks not simply, "What does it mean?" but, "How does it signify?" Multiple valences and a multiple convergence of meanings which contest in a linguistic space for logic have to be acknowledged as an index of the political economy of expressive culture, but so must its situatedness and embodiedness and embeddedness in a real political context where words make a difference about who we are and what we understand and to what uses those words will be put. I saw that operating in the black church in terms of spiritual and moral differences, and I've now taken that lesson seriously in the so-called secular arena. We have to take Derrida seriously; we have to take Foucault seriously when he talks about the insurrection of subjugating knowledges and the ways in which those knowledges make possible different articulative moments within African-American expressive culture and writing. Also, I think we've got to baptize them, as I've tried to argue. I think that the baptism of Derrida or Foucault or Guattari or Baudrillard or Deleuze doesn't mean that we have a narrow nation-state articulation of the logic of American democracy or nationalism—that is, make them show passports because we Americans demand that foreigners genuflect before the altar of American identity. No. It simply means that we have to take the lesson of shading and of creating a discursive frame that allows the particularities and resonances of *this* soil, of the American and, in my case, the African-American soil to dirty language, to dirty theory, to make more gritty the realities that so smoothly travel from European culture to American theory, especially as they are applied to African-American culture. Language is in itself a metaphor of the extraordinary capacity of identities to be shaped and reshaped, of the incredible convergences of different and simultaneous meanings of life that in some senses claim space within both our intellectual and moral worlds and the ways in which those of us who are writers, artists, and intellectuals have to appreciate the extraordinary power that language continues to have especially in minority communities and in oppressed communities where language becomes an index of one's own status. It becomes an index of one's own attempt to create oneself against the world and to say to the world, "I *do* exist." That's why, for me, instances of certain hip-hop culture have been incredibly important in mediating that reality, especially for young black men and women who have been marginalized, not only within the larger white society and mainstream culture, but who have been marginalized even within African-American culture. Those linguistic divisions in black society continue to index deeper class divisions that we have not paid sufficient attention to.

Q. How do you see the transition between academic discourse and more public discourses affecting your work? Are there problems of translation when moving between discourses?

A. I see the transition from the academic to the public as a self-conscious decision to intervene in debates and conversations that happen in public spheres (a different public sphere from the academy because I consider the academy a public sphere) and that have enormous consequence on everyday people's lives. The transition, however, is not smooth; the demands for rigorous debate within the academy are much different from those demands in the public sphere. There are enormous debates going on right now about the function of academized language. I'm not one who—for obvious reasons, self-interest being the primary one [laughter]—jumps on academics because they don't speak for a public audience or because they cannot speak in ways that are clear and articulate. Those are loaded terms: *clear, articulate*. As many other scholars—Henry Giroux, Donna Haraway—have all reminded us, language has multiple functions even within a limited context. To understand that is to acknowledge that there are a variety of fronts upon which we must launch our linguistic and rhetorical resistance against political destruction, against moral misery, and against narrow conceptions of what language does and how it functions. Being reared in a black church, being reared in a so-called minority linguistic community that had rich resources that were concealed and obscured for a variety of reasons, I think that I'm sensitive to the claim against academics and probably understand their defensiveness when they say, "We're writing for a specific audience." That's fine. If you write an article that will be read by a thousand people and those thousand people gain something from it, there's an exchange of information, there's an exchange of ideas, there's a sharpening of the debate, there's a deepening of the basis upon which we understand a particular intellectual subject. There's no reason to be apologetic for that because that's a very specific function within a larger academic enterprise that needs to be undertaken.

If, for instance, somebody writes an essay on a specific aspect of Foucault's appropriation of Benthamite conceptions of the prison that makes clear the relationship between Bentham and Foucault and also rearticulates our conceptions of the panopticon and how surveillance operates as it's extended into the black ghetto, that's all for the good—even if only a thousand people understand the language in which it's deployed and if only they get it. That means that some advance in understanding and exchange of information has gone on, and that's a legitimate enterprise. We don't have a problem with brain surgeons who speak languages that only twelve people can understand. If the man or woman can save your life, speak the jargon; do what you've got to do; operate! So, I don't have a problem with the similar kind of precise, rigorous uses of language that happen in academic circles. The problem arises when hostility is directed against those who are able to take the information, to take the knowledge, to take the profound rigor that is often suggested in such exercises and make them available to a broader audience.

Now, necessarily giving up something in terms of depth for breadth is inevitable. I've written for *Cultural Studies* and *Cultural Critique* and journals that four or five thousand people may read, and I've written for forums that a million and a half and two million people have read. We have to respect the genre. We, as academics, have a deep hostility to those who are public; those who are public intellectuals are viewed as sell-outs. We have our own version of the authentic academic and the authentic intellectual. Authenticity is quite interestingly debated, not only within African-American circles, but within academic circles where people have their narrow conception of what the authentic intellectual is. Interestingly enough, from the late '80s with Russell Jacoby's book on the last intellectual, this debate has been fiercely fought, and interestingly enough around the black public intellectual. I think some of that hostility may be racially coded, but a lot of that hostility is coded in terms of these rigid territorial disputes. A kind of geography of destiny is linked to whether you occupy the terrain of the academy specifically as an academic. We love to talk about transgressions intellectually, academically, but we don't want to do it physically or epistemologically.

Q. Are there any criticisms of your work that you'd like to address?

A. There have been some insightful criticisms of my work. For instance, people were quite interested in *Reflecting Black*. This book of cultural criticism was one of the first that tried to join both theoretical acuity with pop cultural expression and to try to take those two forms—interrogation and expression—seriously in the same text. But at the same time, there was a sacrifice of a certain sort of intellectual acuity. I think that there is a risk involved in trying to join and fuse genres. I wanted to take that risk because I don't want to have a limited audience. I want to speak to the academy in very powerful and interesting ways, but I don't want to be limited to the academy. I know people who limit themselves to the academy, and the academy becomes exaggerated in its importance in their lives. As a Christian who was taught to be suspicious of any form of idolatry, I don't want to make a fetish of critical consciousness. I don't want to make an idol of the capacity to intervene intellectually in the world and make that my entire life and the academy the shrine wherein I worship. At the same time, I want to have a mode of criticism that allows me to be mobile, to move from the academy to the street to the world. I want to be able to speak to that world, and I want to have a language that is clear—with all the problematic implications of clarity. I want to have the ability to be eloquent and clear and powerful and persuasive because I've got a point to make, and I have a point of view. That point of view is worth more to me than what rewards I can reap in the academy; it's about making a difference in the lives of people I meet and whose lives I intend to represent in my work, even if they disagree with much of what I say. Black poor people, black working-class people, black kids who are being demonized as nihilistic animals, black kids who are seen as somehow extraneous, unnecessary to America—I want to speak for and with them. I want to speak for intellectuals who feel that because they're theoretically dense and sophisticated that they have nothing to say. I want to talk about the need to read those books and to struggle with them; anything worth knowing is worth knowing in a very difficult way. I would say to that criticism, I may not do it as well as it needs to be done, but I don't think that the project of trying to fuse those two genres is itself indictable.

There are also more harsh criticisms by people like Adolph Reed. That kind of vitriolic criticism is a sort of vicious gangsta rap in the guise of the academy, not even having the integrity of gangsta rappers who import all forms of signification and tropes and metaphors that indicate that they are not literally true, that they are engaging in a kind of metaphysical realm and a metaphorical world that collides on occasion. They are really artificially invoking an arena of experience that even though real in the world, they themselves realize that they're removed from it; they are thinking about, rapping about, speaking about, something that they know they are once removed from. So they use *bitch* and *whore*; they use *gangsta* and *nigger* in all kinds of interesting ways. But there's a kind of literalism about Adolph Reed that is quite disturbing and destructive—or scholars of that ilk, such as Eric Lott. What is interesting to me about Eric Lott is that he feels free as a white scholar to use words like *troglodyte* and *caveman* and *middlebrow imbecilism* in regard to a work. I think he's a very smart, sophisticated guy who knows the historic contingency of racial rhetoric and who knows the traditional content of racial rhetoric assigned to tropes and metaphors that analyze black people. I would have thought he would have been a bit more careful about associating that—not that he had to worry about some PC police that would rigidly restrict his rhetoric, but that he would be more cautious about the historical inferences of race in assigning certain tropes and metaphors to a person's work. That doesn't in any way take away from the legitimacy of his criticism of my work as not being leftist enough, that by being involved in the public sphere you have to sacrifice certain radical dimensions. This kind of more-leftist-than-thou criticism has a limit in a way: in itself, it becomes cannibalistic. Authors feed off one another to prove that they are more leftist than the next person, and yet the political consequences of that kind of work is only to enhance the scholar's position. It has no consequences on the material effects of the lives of people that they claim they speak for more powerfully than a person like myself: poor black people, poor working-class white people, working-class people, and so on, or even radicals and progressives.

I think I've learned much from people who have taken issue with my work, who have said that there are certain sacrifices that one makes when one moves from the academy into the public sphere, and I think that's absolutely right. But my answer would be: then, you've got to do work for the academy that is important and that is integral to the perpetuation and production of scholarly, academic work; but you've also got to do work that is accountable to a public, that also stands in need of the rich traditions of intellectual reflection that we can bring to bear upon those subjects. And my own mediating position between the academy and the public sphere may never diminish the tension that I feel in terms of traversing those terrains and going back and forth. I hope I won't lose that tension, because I think that tension in some ways informs and gives my work a certain moral authority and hopefully an intellectual integrity that, if not always right, at least is always intending to reflect those tensions in ways that help both the academy and the so-called public sphere. The public sphere needs the intellectual acuity of the academic world. The academic world needs the doses of material consequences and political effects that the public sphere can bring about. That's what I intend to do in my work: to bridge the gulf, to fuse the genres, to swerve between the genres, and to do something really powerful in asking questions about how we can move beyond narrow disciplinary boundaries and narrow divisions between the "real" and the represented and get to the heart of the matter, which is to use powerfully clear work and to serve as a political interest that can be morally defended.

❦ ❦ ❦

Stanley Fish (1991)

Q. Do you consider yourself a writer?

A. I do in some ways. Last night at the Milton Society of America banquet I spoke of the influence on me of C.S. Lewis. I think of

C.S. Lewis and J.L. Austin as the two stylists I've tried to imitate in a variety of ways, and so I'm very self-conscious about the way I craft sentences. I always feel that once I get a particular sentence right I can go on to the next, and I don't go on to the next until I think it's right. In the sense that this is not just superficially but centrally a concern, I consider myself a writer. In other senses— for example, whether I expect people to be studying my works long after my demise—the answer is that I do *not* consider myself a writer. But the craft I think of myself as practicing is the craft of writing, and my obsession there is a very old-fashioned one, a canonical one, a traditional one—and that is clarity.

Q. Would you tell us about your writing process?

A. I do not use a computer and I do not revise. I now use one of those small electronic typewriters that you can move around and take on so-called vacations. That's about as far as I've advanced in the age of mechanical reproduction. Since my writing practices are as I just described, I don't tend to revise. I go back occasionally and reposition an adverb, and I often go through my manuscripts and cross out what I know to be some of my tics. For example, I use the phrase *of course* too much, I often double nouns and verbs for no particular reason, and I have other little favorite mannerisms that I've learned to recognize and eliminate. But very rarely do I ever restructure an essay or even a paragraph.

I write slowly. My pace is two pages a day when I'm writing well, when I have a sense of where the particular essay is or should be going. That's often when I sit for six to eight hours and am continually engaged in the process of thinking through the essay. Also, I do this often (not always, but often) while watching television. This is a very old habit. Actually, this is a talent (if it is a talent) that more people of the younger generation have today than people of my generation. But I've always been able to do it. To this day when I reread something I've written I can remember what television program I was watching when I wrote it. I remember once when I was in Madrid and went to the bullfights, I wrote a passage about Book Six of *Paradise Lost*; every time I look at it I remember that I was watching the bullfights when I wrote it.

I've been strongly influenced as a prose stylist, as I've already mentioned, by C.S. Lewis and J.L. Austin. In fact, I've been very much influenced by J.L. Austin in my thinking about a great many things in addition to my thinking about how to write certain kinds of English sentences. I've also been influenced by Augustine. It's a curious question to answer because many of the people whom I now regularly cite in essays are people that I read *after* most of the views that found my work were already formed. That is, I hadn't read Kuhn before 1979. I'm fond of citing Kuhn, as a great many other people are. I have found support again and again in the pages of Wittgenstein, but I cannot say that it was a study of Wittgenstein that led me to certain questions or answers.

Let me say one more thing. When I was first starting out as a teacher, I gave the same exam in every course, no matter what the subject matter. The exam was very simple: I asked the students to relate two sentences to each other and to the materials of the course. The first sentence was from J. Robert Oppenheimer: "Style is the deference that action pays to uncertainty." I took that to mean that in a world without certain foundations for action you avoid the Scylla of prideful self-assertion, on the one hand, and the Charybdis of paralysis, on the other hand, by stepping out provisionally, with a sense of limitation, with a sense of style. The other quotation, which I matched and asked the students to consider, is from the first verse of Hebrews Eleven: "Now faith is the substance of things hoped for, the evidence of things not seen." I take that to be the classically theological version of Oppenheimer's statement, and so the question of the relationship between style and faith, or between interpretation and action and certainty, has been the obsessive concern of my thinking since the first time I gave this test back in 1962 or 1963. I think there is *nothing* in my work that couldn't be generated from those two assertions and their interactions. They came from a book I used in my composition teaching from the very beginning, and I don't even know how I came to use it. The essays in that book were perhaps the most powerful influence on me. It's a book edited by Walker Gibson, and it's called *The Limits of Language*. It had this essay by Oppenheimer; essays by Whitehead, Conant, and Percy Bridgman, the Nobel Prize winning physicist; Gertrude Stein's essay on punctuation (which is fantastic); and several others that I used in my classes and that informed my early questionings and giving of answers. That book was an extraordinarily powerful influence. Of course, the quotation from Hebrews Eleven came in from my Milton work.

Q. The concept of rhetoric is very important to your work.

A. Substantial realities are products of rhetorical, persuasive, political efforts. When discussing these matters with committed foundationalists, of whom there are still huge numbers, one always is aware that for them the notion of rhetoric only makes sense as a category of inferiority in relation to something more substantial. For someone who listens with a certain set of ears, the assertion of the primacy of rhetoric can only be heard either as an evil gesture in which "the real" is being overwhelmed, or as a gesture of despair in which either a hedonistic amorality or paralysis must follow. All of these responses to the notion of the persuasiveness of rhetoric are, of course, holding on for dear life to a paradigm in which the rhetorical only enters as the evil shadow of the real. If, on the other hand, you begin with a sense of the constructed nature of human reality (one leaves the ontological question aside if one has half a brain), then the notion of the rhetorical is no longer identified with the ephemeral, the outside, but is reconceived as the medium in which certainties become established, in which formidable traditions emerge, are solidified, and become obstacles (not insurmountable ones, but nevertheless obstacles) to the force of counter-rhetorical movements.

Stanley Fish (2000)

Q. A decade ago, I asked you if you considered yourself a writer. Do
you still think of yourself as a writer?

A. Yes, I think of myself as a writer, and as I may have said the last
time we talked, everything for me centers on the sentence. I derive
a great deal of pleasure when I come across a sentence, written by
anyone, that seems well-turned or to do its job. I've found that in
a lot of writing—not only academic writing, but in a lot of writing
these days—there's not much of an ability to handle sentences
crisply. I just admire that, as I assume watchmakers admire certain
things about the movements of fine timepieces, and it's with this
same kind of appreciation of "craft" that I think about a lot of
things in general. It always impresses and pleases me (it's almost
a combination of aesthetic and moral pleasure) when I see
someone who is doing his or her job well. He or she knows what
the job is about and performs it well. And this could be anything:
you may walk into a restaurant and get a sense that the people there
are able to command their profession and to perform its obliga-
tions almost effortlessly and in a way that you hadn't noticed until
you started comparing it with all the other, unhappy experiences
you've had in restaurants. Or it might be the way someone drives
a car, or the way a commercial enterprise is operated.

My writing process has changed [in the last decade] in that I
now use a computer; that's the big change. I had two New Year's
resolutions that I actually kept (I think it was in 1997). I don't
recall any other occasion when I kept a New Year's resolution.
One was to finish a Milton book that I had been working on since
1973. The other was to get online. I did them both, in part
because I had a semester that spring at the National Humanities
Center in Research Park, North Carolina that allowed me to
write a very lengthy introductory chapter of close to a hundred
pages. I decided I would do it on this new instrument that I had
gotten. I had the usual kinds of entry-level problems, but they

all passed and now I'm just like anybody else.

It is true that I don't revise much. I write a couple of pages a day, except when I reach a point where everything seems to be unfolding. This happened actually last week. I was writing a paper on academic freedom and Holocaust denial for a conference later this fall. I wrote perhaps seven or eight pages last Sunday and then finished it off. But that's very unusual.

Q. How do you envision your audience when you are writing?

A. I envision my audience as made up of people who are well educated, in the sense that they're accustomed to reading materials that are about substantive and perhaps even philosophical issues, but who may not be professionally involved with those issues. Therefore, I always think of my audience as a group of persons who should be helped along, not because they are in any way deficient in intelligence or acumen but because they're not inside some of these topics in a professional manner. There's a difference between addressing that audience and, say, going to an American Association of Law Schools meeting and appearing on a panel about the First Amendment. You know that everybody in the audience can recite all of the cases just as you can and refers to them in shorthand, just as movie critics refer to movies in shorthand or Shakespeareans refer to "the Scottish play." That audience is a very specialized one. The audience that might read what I write in a magazine or in an op-ed piece in the *Times* is a different kind of audience in that you have to explain a bit more of the background context—not so that you can bring them up to speed, but so that you can make use of the intelligence they have by not putting them behind an eight ball from the very beginning.

Q. Does the fact that lately you are addressing a general audience mean that you are becoming more of a "public intellectual"?

A. I don't think so. I have a nice relationship with the *New York Times,* which asks me to do op-ed pieces more often than I'm able to do them. I don't come up with ideas that often, and sometimes when an idea is suggested to me, the topic doesn't strike me as something that I really have anything interesting to say about. I don't believe that I'm in the position of commentators like, let's say, Gary Wills or Christopher Hitchens or Dinesh D'Souza or others who are on National Public Radio and various panel talk shows all of the time. I'll do something like that perhaps two or three times a year. Maybe when a book comes out and there's a set of interviews there will be more appearances, but the people who I think are really deserving of the title "public intellectuals" are interacting with the larger public much more often than I am.

Q. So frequency is the key then.

A. Frequency is one key. There's also the sense with people like Gary Wills and the others that I've named that there is a huge number of topics on which they might be commenting. I'm thinking of Norman Ornstein of the American Enterprise Institute and a whole bunch of people like that whose names are recognizable and whose expertise, at least as presented in their columns or magazine pieces, seems much wider than mine.

Q. Do your administrative duties impinge substantially on your scholarly productivity?

A. No, actually not. That is, *The Trouble with Principle* was finished during the first half-year I was here. The Milton book was put together and revised extensively last spring. There have been several essays—such as the one on Holocaust denial, one on Herbert, and one on Marvell—that have now been published. I've written some other pieces in the legal arena, including one called

"Theory Minimalism," which I quite like. So it goes on. The reason is that I've been fortunate all my life to be able to work efficiently. You know the phrase "to turn on a dime"? If there's an hour and I'm on a plane or in a train station, I'll pull out a couple of essays or articles or something that I know I need to work on and I will start planning something. I don't seem to need what a lot of people do need: that space of preparation where you get yourself ready to work, and the light has to be right, and there can't be noise, and so on. I've never had that problem. So I guess what it amounts to is that for me focusing is something that can happen almost instantaneously when I get the opportunity—you know, a little bit of time. It works out quite well that way.

Q. How would you describe your legacy, your contribution to English studies?

A. Well, I think that the essays and books on Milton, Herbert, Donne, Marvell, Jonson, Burton, and Bacon are still doing work in their fields—that is, in the communities that I addressed when I wrote them. And I think that for a while at least (who can put a date on it?) that interpretive work will still be found either helpful or an obstacle to understanding; therefore we must engage it. Now, I'm not sure about the other work, the work on legal theory or First Amendment theory or general interpretive theory or pragmatist theory or reader response theory—I'm not sure. I think that the advantage I might have over some others who address the same questions is the accessibility of my writing, that people do not feel when they read my work that they are required to learn an entirely new vocabulary or have a special dictionary made up. That means that you can assign it to students, who may not find it easy going in some ways but who will not find it full of technical terms that prove to be obstacles to them. So in that sense I think that the style of the writing might give it a chance to be around for a while.

Another thing that can happen to you (you cannot engineer this) is that you can be put "on the list," as I like to put it. By "the list" I mean that everybody writes shorthand accounts of this and that: "cite three or four names that stand for *X*." If you get onto that list, that means that you're going to be around for a little while. So, I may be around if I'm on the list, as I sometimes am with Rorty, Kuhn, Derrida, or whomever. A couple weeks ago, Jim Atlas wrote a piece about Al Gore's reading habits in which he wonders why Gore doesn't read Derrida and me. I think there are very good answers to that question, but, you see, what I'm saying is that the *name* and therefore to some extent the *work* achieves a certain currency that is entirely an accident of rolodexes. (I happen to know Jim Atlas, but that's irrelevant to the point.) When people are searching for a few names to put on the list that would be identified either as, let's say, "cutting-edge," or as "enemies of civilization," then I—not always, but sometimes—will be one of those names. But I didn't do that. That's just the fact that there were some newspaper and magazine pieces twelve or thirteen years ago, and then the set of names to which you might refer in shorthand to make a point is solidified by journalists—and there I am. It's bizarre in a lot of ways because usually I'm there in ways that are totally inaccurate: Fish the relativist. Actually, the best that I've seen recently (and I wrote a little bit about this) was in *Heterodoxy*, which is David Horowitz's journal. There was a piece in it—it must have been in January or February, 2000—in which I am referred to as a communist! I thought, this is really something! As a communist! So it's that kind of thing—where your name becomes something that people can just plop into a sentence and put next to a noun or an adjective without any strong sense of what any of the writing is like.

❧ ❧ ❧

Paulo Freire

Q. Do you consider yourself a writer?

A. The other day a friend of mine asked me, "Paulo, do you think that
sometime you could become a member of some academy of
letters?" I said, "No." And he asked me, "But why? Do you have
some prejudice?" I said, "No, I don't; it's just that I don't feel that
I'm a writer." I would like very much to be a writer. Of course,
when I publish books this is because I write good books. I write
essays; I write about my *praxis*; I write about philosophy and the
politics of education, but I don't make "literature." Whether I
write well or not, whether I have good taste—I would like very
much to have good taste in writing—is another question. Yet for
me, this would not be enough to make me a member of an academy
of letters. The novelists, the poets—they are writers for me.
Maybe I'm wrong; maybe I have a narrow understanding of being
a writer. I also have to tell you that in thinking like this I feel sad
because I would like very much to be a writer. Maybe in some
moments of my books—a certain moment of the analysis I am
doing, and so on—readers could think they are reading a "writer."
This is when I become most happy in writing. For example, in one
of my short books that's already in English, *The Importance of
the Act of Reading*, I think that perhaps there are moments that
give the impression that somewhere inside of the educator is a
sleeping writer.

Q. Tell us about your writing habits.

A. I can tell you with humility, with humor, but not with irony, that
I am underdeveloped. I am a man of northeast Brazil, one of the
very precarious regions in the world, and I am almost seventy
years old, so it's difficult to start learning some things, especially

things concerning machines and technology. I believe in my hand, in the pencil, and in the white piece of paper before me. I believe in that. Then I start filling up the paper with my thought and transforming it into words. I don't even know how to type; I never use a typewriter. I am thinking about buying a computer for my wife to use to write her essays, her books—and also for me to use. But I don't believe that I will learn how to use it. It's very sad that the educator Paulo Freire would say such a thing. Yet, I am convinced that all of us need to use computers. I see how my friends in the States—professors such as Ira Shor, Henry Giroux, Donaldo Macedo—produce their work with such discipline. They know how to use the machine, how to put it at their service. It's fantastic. They do much more than I because they use a very good instrument. My friends all tell me, "Paulo, you have to learn to use the computer." And maybe I will start, because I believe that in the last analysis there's always time for us to learn.

Q. In some of your publications, you have attempted to transcend the constraints of conventional text formats by experimenting with various dialogic forms. *Pedagogy in Process* is a collection of letters that together constitute a dialogue between you and revolutionary leader Mario Cabral; even the introduction is, in your words, a "letter-report" to the reader. *Learning to Question* is what you've called "a spoken book," a lengthy conversation between you and Antonio Faundez. And *A Pedagogy for Liberation* is a collection of "dialogues" between you and Ira Shor. Why have you found these experimental formats necessary?

A. Maybe before I perceived them as *necessary*, I saw them as *possible*. I remember that one day some years ago—in the 1980s, maybe '81 or '82—I asked myself, "Why not start *speaking* books instead of exclusively *writing* them?" Of course, I never thought that we should stop writing in favor of speaking books, but why not do the two things from time to time, and even simultaneously? Then I invited a young Brazilian educator from São Paulo to make the first experience with me. He accepted, and we started a dialogue, following a certain thematic issue, and we spoke a book entitled *On Education*. Immediately, we did a second volume, and afterwards we started another. Today, I think I have five or six such books, some of them very good ones. The book with Ira Shor is for me excellent, not because of *me* but because of *us*. Ira is very critical, very lucid, and the book is very good. In every language, the book has had a good reception. And *Learning to Question*, with the Chilean philosopher Antonio Faundez, is also for me a very good book. I did that, as I said, not because I thought it should be done, but because I thought that it *could* be done, that it was possible to do.

❦ ❦ ❦

Clifford Geertz

Q. In what ways do you think of yourself as a writer?

A. In all kinds of ways. I started out to *be* one; that's the first answer. I wanted to be a novelist and a newspaper man. As an undergraduate, I had the notion—maybe an antiquated one by now—that one could work on a newspaper and write novels in the evening. I went to Antioch College and majored in English, at least in the beginning, with the intention of doing something like that. In high school I had edited a newspaper and a literary magazine—the usual sort of thing. So I wanted to be a novelist. I even wrote a novel (though I didn't publish it) and some short stories. Antioch had a co-op program so I went to work for the *New York Post* as a copyboy. Then I decided I didn't want to be a newspaper man; it was fun, but it wasn't practical. After a while I shifted into philosophy as a major, but I never had any undergraduate training at all in anthropology and, indeed, very little social science outside of economics. I had a lot of economics but nothing else. Anthropology wasn't even taught at Antioch then, although it is now. And except for a political science course or two and lots of economics, I didn't have any social sciences. So I was in literature for at least half the time I was there, the first couple of years, and then I shifted to philosophy, partly because of the influence of a terrific teacher and partly because in a small college you can run out of courses. Then I got interested in the same sort of thing I'm interested in now: values, ideas, and so on. Finally, one of my professors said, "Why don't you think about anthropology?" That was the first time I had thought seriously about being an anthropologist, and then I began to think about it and I went to Harvard and so on.

So I came in preformed as a writer and put writing aside for awhile because I had to learn what anthropology was all about and do research and get a kind of union card as a working anthropologist. But, yes, I really am a novelist manqué. (Some of my enemies would say I'm still a novelist—a fiction writer anyway.) So it's not accidental; I've always had that bent, I guess, and I still do. I think of myself as a writer who happens to be doing his writing as an anthropologist. I've often been accused of making anthropology just into literature, but I don't believe I'm doing that. Anthropology is also field research and so on, but writing is central to it.

Q. Would you describe your writing process?

A. I've spent a lot of time in the field—almost a dozen years in Southeast Asia and North Africa—where I don't do any writing at all. I can't write in the field. I write a lot of field notes, but I can't compose anything. I once started to write a book review in the field, but that didn't work. I just can't do it. I think there's a much greater separation in anthropology, especially among field anthropologists, than in a lot of social sciences between the research and the writing—at least as I do it. You do two or two-and-a-half years in Java in which all you do is live with the people, write down everything, and try to figure out what the hell is going on;

then you come back and *write*—out of the notes, out of your memories, and out of whatever is going on in the field. So, for me at least, it's a fairly divided life. I don't write in the field; I write after I return. Mostly, *here* I write and *there* I research.

As far as *how* I write, there's no single answer. I hesitate to confess this in public because I think it's a very bad way to do things, but I'll do it anyway: I don't write drafts. I write from the beginning to the end, and when it's finished it's done. And I write very slowly. That may seem odd, because I've written a lot, but I've often been in situations like this one here in Princeton where I've had a lot of time to write. I never leave a sentence or a paragraph until I'm satisfied with it; and except for a few touch-ups at the end, I write essentially one draft. Once in a while people ask me for early drafts, but these drafts just don't exist. So I just go from line one to line *X*—even in a book. I have an outline, especially if it's a book, but I hardly pay attention to it. I just build it up in a sort of craft-like way of going through it carefully, and when it's done it's done. The process is very slow. I would not advise that other people write this way. I know people who can write a first draft and not care whether it's idiotic. They'll write "blah, blah, blah," and put zeros to hold space for something to be filled in later. Good writers do this. I wish I could too, but for reasons that are probably deeply psychological, it's impossible. I usually write about a paragraph a day, but at least it's essentially finished when it's done. And all of this is not due just to the computer, because I've only used the computer for a year or so. I write by hand; even now I write by hand. I just type text into the computer so I can print it out and read it.

Q. What is it about a given text that makes us take the author and the text seriously?

A. In *Works and Lives* that's a question I *asked* rather than tried to give a definitive answer to. So my first response is that I don't know. If you look in anthropology, the diversity of kinds of texts that have been persuasive and have had purchase in the field militates against any simple conclusion. In *Works and Lives*, I really wasn't trying to establish a canon; rather, I was trying to say, "This seems to be the canon; why do we believe Evans-Pritchard and Lévi-Strauss and Malinowski and Benedict and some others?" I think the answer to your question is itself empirical, and I think it's empirical in a discipline that is yet to come—that is, rhetorical analysis in anthropology. We need to think more about the nature of rhetoric in anthropology, and that's what I tried to begin. There isn't a body of knowledge and thought to fall back on in this regard.

I think people *are* making judgments about what constitutes persuasive writing, but I don't think they know what basis they're making them on. In recent years, there's been more and more writing about anthropological writing, but still there's not that much. . . . It certainly is true that just the assembly of facts is not going to make a text persuasive; if it were, there would be a lot of very dull books that would be a lot more famous than they are. Somehow, the sense of circumstantiality and of power in reserve (if an anecdote or an example doesn't sound strained but sounds like you've got fifty others and this is the best one you chose) are factors that are rhetorically important. I guess I want to dodge the issue, mostly because I just don't know the answer.

What I want to see get started is a lot more reflection about these matters. Book reviews in *The American Anthropologist* hardly ever concern themselves with rhetoric. The most you ever hear is, "It's well written," or "It's lousily written," or "It's obscure," but no real sense of how the book is put together. You almost never get anything about how composition occurs, how the text is constructed, how the argument is developed, and why it is or isn't persuasive. There's very little about "writing" in that sense. So we're operating in the dark. Yet at the same time, and this is what started me with the kinds of concerns addressed in *Works and Lives*, there's a fair consensus in the field about what the canonical books are. We aren't in that much of a debate about them. We may like or not like what *A* or *B* says, but nobody is going to say that Lévi-Strauss is not an important anthropologist or that Evans-Pritchard or Malinowski wasn't influential. Most people would say that these are significant people. But we just don't know *why* their works are persuasive. . . .

It is odd in anthropology, because if you read a book by me on Java or some other place, you either take it or leave it. You don't know anything about the place. You could read another couple of books and probably get more confused, but there's no way of matching it to "reality." (If the correspondence theory of truth ever does work, it doesn't work here.) If I write about the Balinese cockfight, who knows what's what? A few readers might be able to make *some* comparisons, but the average reader is just left with the text and with what I'm saying about the subject. So why the cockfight piece has been popular, why that took hold, is interesting to me. Why certain papers, certain articles, certain pieces, certain books, certain writers have a kind of persuasiveness, why we believe them, is curious. . . . If there's ever a place where you *can't* argue that you can put the facts over here and the text over there and see if they fit, it is surely in anthropology.

And it won't be persuasive if the writer's side is missing either. There are lots of "literary" books (in the bad sense) in anthropology that nobody believes because readers just don't feel the writer really understands what the X indians or the Y natives are all about, and they feel, therefore, that the text is in the bad sense a "fiction." On the other hand, it *has to be* something of a fiction: it has to be *made*; it has to be *constructed*. That's the mule image that I gave. We have to be both of those things. That's what interests me about the Barthes distinction; he was concerned at least somewhat with this problem. [In *Works and Lives*, Geertz speaks of "the North African mule who talks always of his mother's brother, the horse, but never of his father, the donkey" as an example of how we suppress parts of our heritage "in favor of others supposedly more reputable."]. . . .

Generally, I'm not wildly experimental, but my own writings in anthropology are certainly nonstandard. They're not wild or off the edge of the map or anything, but they aren't the way most anthropologists write. And certainly when I started they weren't. There are more people doing it now.

Q. Your writings are nonstandard because they're not part of the conventional discourse of the discipline?

A. Yes. There's been mimicry of the sciences in an attempt to sort of be fashioned after them—you write an introduction, then the findings, then the conclusions. I've written—not only I but more and more other people have written—in a much more off-the-wall sort of way in an attempt, among other things, to cope with that endless dilemma of not making the Balinese or the Moroccans or the Javanese sound like they live on the moon but also not making them sound like they live next door. They don't do either of those things. To cope with that dilemma I think some sort of experiments in prose are necessary, some sort of departure from received canons of description.

There are people who write much less standard discourse than I do. Some of the people to the intellectual left feel that I'm still writing linear prose, which they see as a big mistake. (I should be putting things in all capital letters and that kind of thing.) I don't think necessarily that nonstandard prose is always better than standard prose or standard writing. I just think that in anthropology and the social sciences the received canons are limiting. So yes, I do think it's something that goes on all the time, and it goes on in degrees. Every once in a while, somebody really revolutionizes the way things are done; most of the time, they inch up on it and after a while you notice that it's really done in quite a different way than it was before. It's always amusing to look at how something early in the twentieth century was written in anthropology and how it's written now. You can see that somehow there's been an enormous shift in how it's done, but yet you can't put your finger on someone who actually did this—there's no Joyce, for example.

Q. You write that the "establishment of an authorial presence within a text has haunted ethnography from very early on. . . . Finding somewhere to stand in a text that is supposed to be at one and the same time an intimate view and a cool assessment is almost as much of a challenge as gaining the view and making the assessment in the first place."

A. Actually, most of that kind of problem has centered on the question we usually refer to as "reflexivity." In *Works and Lives* I have some sardonic things to say about some attempts in that direction, though I think it's the direction to move. It's very hard to do this. On the other hand, a recent book by Renato Rosaldo talks, in terms that I think are better than reflexivity, of the "positioned observer." At least in the kind of anthropology that I and people like Renato and others do—as I've said, there are lots of kinds of anthropology—we are part of what we study, in a way; we're there. And it seems to me almost in a kind of positivist sense *false* not to represent ourselves as being so—false, or at least an imperfect representation. Now, I've never done it. Well, in the piece on religion in Java and in the cockfight piece and in a few other pieces I'm there, I'm self-represented; once in a while I've done it. But I've never really thoroughly done it, and I've written a lot of books which are written from the moon—the view from nowhere. I am persuaded that at least for some works, for a lot of works, we've really got to get ourselves back into the text, to have ourselves truly represented in the text. I've always argued that in part I'm represented in my texts by my style, that at least people won't think my books were written by anybody else, that there's a kind of signature in them. But I think Renato is right: we have to go further than that; we have to situate ourselves within the text. In the book I'm writing now, *After the Fact*, *that's* what I'm trying to do. It's not confessional anthropology, and it's not about what I was feeling or something of that sort; it's trying to describe the work I've been doing with myself in the picture.

Q. So you're going back to your earlier pieces and analyzing them?

A. I'm going back to my whole career—not the pieces so much, just to the work—and trying to reconceptualize it in these terms. I'm trying to restate it as work that was done by human hands—that is, *mine*. As I say, I think in my earlier work there are places where this occurs, and in my writing style even more so; but I think one needs to go further, and the whole problem is that it's very difficult to do. Now, I don't like confessional anthropology. Part of the confessional anthropology came out of the sixties when, for example, I had a hard time convincing students that they were going to North Africa or someplace to understand the North Africans, not to understand themselves. I'm in favor of people understanding themselves, and that's in a certain way what anthropology's about; but you really want to know what the *Moroccans* are like, and I still do that. That's what my vocation seems to be to me. But these people are right (as I say, thinking on these lines has advanced a bit) that you can't do that as though you were, again, on the moon. We need to find ways of bringing ourselves in. There are different ways to do it, and there are some silly ways to do it. . . . I think it's something, getting back to writing, that we don't know how to do rhetorically. We don't know how to do it effectively. We're getting better, perhaps, and there are some successes and some failures and some semi-successes. In any case, what I'm doing now is that I'm really trying to see whether I *can* do it unawkwardly. But it's a writing task, as far as I'm concerned. . . .

This is again Renato's notion of the positioned scholar. You *are* somebody: you come out of a certain class; you come out of a certain place; you go into a certain country; you then go home; you do *all* of these things. To represent it as though it were a laboratory study of some sort, in the traditional sense, seems to me to misrepresent it. So the expectations that have been formed, and that have been formed by ethnographic writers, that the anthropologist is not involved in what's going on, are false. It's not really a veridical picture, in a very simple sense of *veridical*, of what anthropological research is all about. How you undo that preoccupation with a sense of distance and so on is difficult to know. More and more people are trying, especially the younger group.

Henry Giroux

Q. Do you consider yourself a writer?

A. I have always wanted to write, not because I wanted to view myself as a writer but because writing offered me an opportunity both to engage in public issues and to participate in broader public dialogues. Of course, as a child I was a terrible writer because I lacked the kind of middle-class education that provides one with the skills and cultural capital necessary to write. My primary mode of communication was oral, local, and experiential. Writing was viewed with disdain by my friends and myself because it was used in school to punish working-class kids; it was used both as a weapon and as a sorting device to label us and to sort us out from our middle-class peers. It took me a long time to get over the feeling of inferiority I carried around regarding my inability to write and express myself in written language. I actually didn't start writing seriously until I was around thirty years old. Unfortunately, once I started I couldn't stop, and I guess one could argue that I got a bit carried away with writing after that. But writing did more that take me out of my working-class neighborhood and allow me to speak to many audiences and extend the meaning of what it means to make one's pedagogy more public. It also allowed me to define myself as something other than a traditional academic, which always conjured up for me a kind of professional posturing defined through the degraded ritual of being disinterested, specialized, apolitical, and removed from public life. Writing allowed me to break out of the academic microcosm, take sides, fight for a position, push against the grain, and say unsettling things—all those attributes that make one "un-cool," as one of my colleagues recently suggested of those of us who avoid the cleverness of academic posturing and happen to believe that intellectuals actually have some public responsibilities in fashioning a politics of resistance and hope. I agree completely with Arundhati Roy, who argues that writing imposes on authors an intricate web of morality, rigor, and responsibility, and in doing so works to reclaim the primacy of a politics in which one addresses the possibilities for deepening the promise of democratic struggles. At this point, I do consider myself a writer, but not in a literary or aesthetic sense. I see myself more as an engaged writer, a border crosser from the working-class who can struggle on many fronts, build upon the work of others, and do my best to analyze, challenge, and, hopefully with others, overcome the imposed silences of power and normalized common-sense understandings of dominant orthodoxies, and do so from the perspective of a kind of militant utopianism. At the same time, writing offers me the opportunity for engaging politics as a crucial pedagogical and cultural task.

Q. Would you describe your writing process.

A. In this age of high-speed technologies and instant messaging, I sometimes have to remind myself that I wrote two books not with a computer but with a ballpoint pen. I remember sitting at my desk, endlessly tearing pages out of a pad and throwing them on the floor as I would revise and revise whatever I was writing. Revising is a passion for me: everything I write must go through more drafts than I can even remember. The computer has made the revising process easier for me, though I still revise extensively. But by "revising" I don't just mean rewriting the text as much as I mean rethinking and reworking ideas. Moreover, I have my wife Susan (who is a much better writer than I am) read and comment on everything I write—and then its back to more revisions. My early drafts are always painful and usually pretty bad. I find myself quite depressed at the beginning of the writing process, and it is only later after many revisions that the work seems to get better, making me feel a bit more confident that I actually may have something to say that is worth reading and making public.

Q. What is the easiest part of writing for you?

A. The easiest part of writing is recognizing a topic that interests me. My writing is drawn from a particular way of reading the world and is fueled by the problems and contradictions I see emerging out of that world. Some things just stand out because of the urgency of the problem, and I never know where the issue is going to take me or how I am going to develop it, but once the issue hits me, it is like getting an adrenaline shot and I feel both excited and utterly connected to the world. I both enjoy and am terribly excited at that stage of the work. My work has always been driven by public issues and projects, and the nature of that connection allows me both to write and to be in the world in a way that exceeds both traditional definitions of being a writer and being an academic as well.

Q. What is the hardest part of writing for you?

A. Once I get an idea, the daunting task begins of reading everything I can on the subject, collecting information, data, and trying to think through how the project will be developed. This usually takes me a couple of months, if not much longer, depending on the project. I enjoy the research, but I find that I can't actually think through a project or write anything until I can sequence my argument and see how it is going to be developed. Trying to figure out the sequence is very painful for me, and I usually get very depressed at some point if after months of work the sequence is just not in place for some reason. Once I get the sequence, however, the writing seems to proceed smoothly. The other difficult problem I have is trying to construct a discourse that is accessible without being simplistic, unsettling without being obtuse, and moving without resorting to the pretense of being clever. My writing has changed considerably over the years in that it is much more accessible and appeals to a much wider audience; but, at the same time, I do not think it is any less demanding theoretically or any less rigorous. I find it very difficult to maintain the balance between rigor and accessibility. I have to work very hard to write in a style that appeals to diverse readers and publics but is still capable of intervening in ongoing public conversations and raising important questions, sometimes in a vernacular that may be unfamiliar but hopefully not so as to be uninviting.

Q. Would you describe your method of research for a writing project?

A. I guess every writer invents a personal method of assimilating material and working through ideas, information, and arguments. When I first started writing, I used to put everything down on cards, file them, and then go over them when trying to write. This method failed miserably for me because by the time I finished my research I could barely remember what I had read initially, and simply rereading a number of cards loaded with various ideas just did not prove useful to me. The method I developed over thirty years ago and still use today seemed to solve the problem of working with a short memory and trying to engage a great deal of information and sources in order to do justice to any particular topic. Here's how it works. Whenever I read something, I mark off in the text those paragraphs that contain important organizing ideas. I might circle a paragraph and write an organizing idea in the margins. When I finish the piece, I copy it and go through a cut-and-paste procedure in which I type out the source on the top of a piece of paper, type in the organizing ideas from the piece (article, chapter, and so on), and place the paragraph underneath its respective organizing idea. Hence, I may read a twenty-page piece by, let's say, Fred Jameson. In that piece, I may find fifteen sections that I have marked as important. I then reference the piece, type out the organizing ideas starting with the order in which I read the piece. I then paste the respective paragraphs under the typed heading. In the end, I may end up with a four-page cut-out of Jameson's piece. I then duplicate it so I can have a clean copy and I file the original. When my research is done, I read all of the cut-and-paste articles, one by one, and I write next to each paragraph in each article an organizing idea. I then type out a cover sheet listing all of the organizing ideas for each working article. I then paste all of the cover sheets on artist boards and try to figure out from reading the sheets how I might develop my arguments. The method really works for me. Moreover, I file everything that I cut and paste, and when necessary I can go back and read my notes and familiarize myself with any number of issues, traditions, or theoretical concerns in a short period of time. I must say, though, that after using this method for over twenty-five years, I have more notes that I can possibly ever read.

Stuart Hall

Q. You have described identity as a "production," a "matter of 'becoming' as well as of 'being.'" How does your writing continue to construct your identity? And how does your cultural and historical identity continue to construct you as a writer?

A. The point that I have made about identity is, perhaps, a familiar one, but it is worth restating. It's the notion that identity is always in the making. There is one idea of identity as a fixed position, and another idea that identity is relative to the extreme. There is now a third position in that debate because I think those people have moved away from identity as process and have sometimes gone right over to the point where identity is nothing at all; it's a kind of open field where one just sort of occupies a particular identity out of habit. So it is that there's no fixed identity, but it's not that there's just an open-ended horizon where we can just intentionally choose. What that means is that there is no final, finished identity position or self simply then to be produced by the writing. Any cultural practice plays a role in the construction of identity. While it's true that you may have a very clear notion of what the argument is and that you may be constructing that argument very carefully, very deliberately, your identity is also in part *becoming through the writing*. It's inflected by the very language you use because in order to express something, to occupy language, you are necessarily playing a game—a language game that other people have played and used. Meaning is already sediment in that language, so you reactivate all those other marks of meaning as well as what *you're* trying to say. Of course, writing is also a production, a production of knowledge and a production of a version of the self.

Q. Historically and contextually, at the moment of writing.

A. Yes, exactly. And we therefore occupy our identities very retrospectively: having produced them, we then know who we are. We say, "Oh, that's where I am in relation to this argument and for these reasons." So, it's exactly the reverse of what I think is the common-sense way of understanding it, which is that we already know our "self" and then put it out there. Rather, having put it into play in language, we *then* discover what we are. I think that only then do we make an investment in it, saying, "Yes, I like that position, I am that sort of person, I'm willing to occupy that position." Then it becomes a kind of space of enunciation for further thoughts and a space for other kinds of practices. The reverse is also true: you can produce a self in writing that is not close to a position you want to hold for very long, and others that go off on tangents and don't engage the unconscious.

Q. Do you go back and read your own writing?

A. I do, yes—not to think how wonderful I was, but because I'm not a terribly good editor of my own writing. Three weeks later I will see things wrong with my writing that I didn't see at the time. So that's one kind of rereading. Another kind of rereading is sort of incidental. I've been winding up my work after being at the Open University for seventeen years, so I'm throwing away a lot of paper. I'm really surprised by all kinds of things, particularly a certain kind of recurrence, a certain consistency that I hadn't been aware of. And I say this because I'm not attached to consistency. I don't think it's a terrible thing that I'm saying something different now from what I said in the 1980s. Times have moved on, so why shouldn't one say that? So I'm a bit surprised to find that I still think about class what I thought in the 1960s. It's really quite sad to find out that one doesn't move on, or that one has only five thoughts in a lifetime. [Laughter.] Perhaps there are ten good things you might think in a lifetime and you sort of go on thinking around those same lines. But I am struck by the fact that I have been preoccupied by the same kinds of questions throughout many different kinds of writings, and I only see this retrospectively when I look back at things I've written.

Q. You've written eloquently about Raymond Williams' influence on your own intellectual growth. You've also spoken very specifically about his commitment to using what he called a "shared" vocabulary and about his writing: his style, his ability to address a wider audience than just his immediate peers. How has Williams' writing, as such, influenced your own writing?

A. His is a very distinctive style. He has more than one style, for one thing. He has a style that is directed toward a general public, a general readership rather than a narrowly academic or intellectual one; and he has a more serious, intellectual style that is unique in a number of ways. One is the ability to connect areas and

experiences and structures, as he does with a phrase like "structure of feeling." This is an oxymoron because you know that
structures don't have feelings and feelings don't have structures.
But "structure of feeling of an age" is exactly the intangible ethos
that is the complex, cultural outcome of a variety of different
practices. If you can grasp what the structure of feeling is, grasp
the sort of background, the emotional canvas on which other
debates are taking place, you can perhaps also see that the people
who are opposed in terms of their positions also share something
vital, something immensely important, because they're both part
of that structure of feeling. Although they may oppose one another
in terms of their logical political argument, they also have a basis
for a dialogue. So, Raymond is wonderfully suggestive, and I like
Keywords very much because it's neither a strictly lexicographi-
cal exercise nor an attempt to write a definitive history. Those
things are extraordinarily rich for me in terms of his writing.

Q. In a discursive sense, can we articulate new ways of thinking and
being while using the same terms, the same vocabulary?

A. Exactly. Writing is kind of a game of defining one's terms against
the uses one doesn't want as one goes. Every time I use *ethnicity*
I have to make sure that I'm not being slotted back into the
essentialist notion of ethnicity or what I'm saying could be
completely misunderstood. And there *are* certain misunderstandings, whether deliberate or not, and I rather like that. Both Homi
Bhabha and I use the term *hybridity*, and Robert Young has
accused us both of occupying nineteenth-century racial theory
because *it* uses the term *hybridity*. Of course, I'm not talking about
hybridity in that sense; I'm using it metaphorically. But I have no
other term. I can only take up *that* term, try to refuse its racialist
connotations, and try to reinvest it with a new kind of cultural
meaning. I don't know how else to talk. But you are always open
to exactly that kind of misinterpretation. Someone will always say
that if you're talking about ethnicity you're just in one of the old

ethnics: "America is an ethnically pluralist society, what's wrong with that, we're a melting pot," and so forth. We are trapped by the deconstructive moment in some of the primary concepts with which cultural studies is trying to operate. These are its concepts. Each of them is no longer tenable in terms of an old vocabulary, but we have no entirely new dispensation with which to think. It requires a kind of double operation, rhetorically, discursively, in that one uses terms that are untenable; one occupies a conceptual world but one no longer believes in the translation.

Q. Are there any criticisms or misunderstandings of your work that you'd like to address?

A. You know, I have to say that I don't read criticisms of my work. I have limited time for reading. When I left the Centre for Cultural Studies, I decided that I would contribute in other ways. I participated in compiling a history of cultural studies and of what happened at Birmingham. I don't want to privilege my view over other people's, but I do have a view about what occurred. But when I decided that I wouldn't really participate in the attempt to police the boundaries of cultural studies, what I did was to move to new substantive areas: back into questions of race. I thought it was more important for me to contribute to a particular area of work in cultural studies than to try to be responsible for deciding where the field was going. In the time that I've had available to read, I have preferred to read in the areas in which I'm thinking and writing, to read what others are doing in such areas rather than what others think about me and my work. I've been more interested in reading the debates about ethnicity and postcolonial theory and its developments than in tracking and responding to the criticisms of my own work. This is not a justification for it, and I think it's not a very good practice because people will think I'm disdainful of my critics, but I just don't know the rude things that they're saying because I haven't read them. Occasionally, I do come across criticisms, and I have the usual prickly responses when people misunderstand me. As you could tell by something I said previously, I was very wounded by Robert Young, that someone as sophisticated as he would willfully misunderstand me, would think that because I use the word *hybridity* I am complicit with nineteenth-century racial theory. But there are many other valid criticisms that I would take on board, but I can't. I am sometimes thought to be not very consistent—eclectic, really—for which I've already offered you a sort of an apologia. I think a certain kind of theoretical eclecticism in our period of heady intellectual and theoretical innovation can be a useful strategy. A friend of mine who says he is forever trying to keep up with these intellectual maneuvers asked me once if I thought that if he ducked he could miss the Lacanian moment! [Laughing.] Sometimes I've felt like ducking and that perhaps it would just go away and be over before I'd had to come to grips with it. So, eclecticism may be an excuse for a sort of lazy intellectual practice, a form of skillful intellectual ducking.

I don't think of myself as a theoretician. I don't have a philosophical mind that would allow me to stay at a certain level of abstraction for a long period of time. I can't sustain that. But that works for me because I'm interested in the dialogical relationship between theoretical concepts and the concrete. I put it that way because I'm not an empiricist either. It's not theory or empiricism; it is theory and concrete conjunctures—that's the interface that I find meaningful and productive. I suppose that's why I've remained more of a Gramscian than many other people who started out that way and have since abandoned Gramsci. Gramsci is interesting in exactly that interface between theory and the concrete, material world. So, it's necessary to know what you're good at and not pretend you're good at something else. In terms of my work, then, I've come to recognize that texts are only momentary stabilizations and then you give them back to the flow of meaning. They are appropriated by other people who will take from them what they will regardless of your intent. Every reading of a text is basically a translation, not a transmission of originary truth from one moment to another. One must give them away freely. People quite often get something different—but, you know, I got something different from Gramsci than what he'd intended me to get. I use Derrida in a way that would drive formal deconstructionists wild. My own work—and everyone else's, too—must be surrendered to that flow of meaning that will continue to create and recreate something new of the old.

❦ ❦ ❦

Donna Haraway

Q. Do you consider yourself a writer?

A. "Yes" is the short answer. My coming to think of myself as a writer has grown over the last few years. While at Santa Cruz, I felt that I got permission to consider myself a writer in a way that I hadn't in other academic jobs where the generic conventions of argumentation mitigated against taking writing itself seriously. I was more and more compelled by the physical process of writing, creating a tissue of words; by the kind of quasi-dreamstate that writing puts me (and I think most writers) into; by the experience of working through a sentence and finding that it's committed me to half a dozen positions that I don't hold, literally because of the material density of language; and by finding that writing is itself a material process of thinking, that there's no thinking process outside of some materiality. The particular tissue of writing became more and more interesting as a part of my work. I have friends for whom the injunction to be clear remains right at the top of their moral, epistemological, and political commitments. It's always struck me that the injunction to be clear is a very strange goal because it assumes a kind of physical transparency, that if you could just clean up your act somehow the materiality of writing would disappear. This is a psychological problem, as opposed to exactly what's interesting about working in that medium. So yes, I consider myself a writer, more and more so.

And I've become increasingly more certain that this is part of the substance of *our* work collectively in science studies and that it's not some personal indulgence or some inability to "think clearly."

Q. What distinguishes your notion of "cyborg writing" from traditional phallogocentric, authoritative practices of mastery and domination?

A. Cyborg writing has inherited the kind of acid consciousness of people like Derrida and others who have made it simply impossible to engage in authoritative writing *as if* the subject who did such a thing weren't implicated in the practice and *as if* the history of writing weren't the history of the differentiation of the world for us with all of the sticky threads to questions of power and to whose way of life is at stake in marking up the world that way rather than some other way. That kind of irreducible immersion in writing, that kind of irreducible immersion in worldliness, is what I feel I've inherited from the critical tools of poststructuralism broadly considered. So writing—which is itself a trope and can't carry all the weight for worldly practice—can carry a lot of the weight for worldly practice because it insists on our own implication in meaning-making materiality. When I think of the difference between cyborg writing and the opposition I set up— traditional, phallogocentric, authoritarian, that sort of long list of "bad"—the important issue for me is that the cyborg is from the start a polluted category. It's a truly odd subject position that I took up in a kind of insane, gleeful, critical, angry spirit. It's an offspring of World War II nuclear culture, and there's no possibility of working out of that position to imagine yourself in the Garden of Eden or returning to pre-Oedipal bliss. Many of the myths and narratives are not available to you from what I would call "cyborg positions." You have to take your implication in a fraught world as the starting point. I don't think that's true for authoritative writing practices that try very hard to produce the kind of masterful "I," a particular kind of authority position that makes the viewer forget the apparatus of the production of that authority. I think cyborg writing is resolutely committed to foregrounding the apparatus of the production of its own authority, even while it's doing it. It's not eschewing authority, but it's insisting on a kind of double move, a foregrounding of the apparatus of the production of bodies, powers, meanings. At first, naming it "cyborg" was flip in a way, but then I liked it better and better. Any kid born at the end of World War II—sort of eating the apple in the Atomic Cafe rather than the apple in the Garden of Eden—has to come to terms with the extraordinary role that communication systems and cybernetics plays in our literacy practices. So it was to catch those meanings.

Q. How might those interested in employing literacy as a form of liberation resist the "violent" uses of literacy?

A. First, it's not new that literacy is intimately implicated in projects of domination; this is a very, very old story. You have to tell the origin of writing and the story of domination together, no matter where you decide to start your narrative. So in one sense, I think we're immersed in a very old issue. Literacy projects—the acquisition of the power to mark the world effectively in the various literacies that pertain to the social world we're living in (which in our case certainly still includes writing with paper and pen, but also with keyboard and video screen), the multiple literacies that it takes to build the world into categories that can be livable for you and your people—are freedom projects. And freedom projects return to the history of the importance of reading and writing for colonized people, that kind of seizing of the tools that marked you as other, and to contemporary literacy work: Paulo Freire of the previous generation, who is the inescapable ancestor; the projects of June Jordan, the way she writes about African-American education in the United States; the way Gloria Anzaldúa does literacy work; the way someone like Theresa Hak Kyung Cha, the really interesting Korean American via the Francophone world, does writing; the way Katie King at the University of Maryland talks about feminism and writing projects and the sort of layerings of locals and globals in writing projects; the way Romona Fernandez at Sacramento City College writes about "trickster literacy." You can't talk about the history of contemporary liberation struggles without talking about joining freedom projects and literacy projects. So there's not a simple opposition between writing as a tool of domination and liberation. [In this regard,] I think of Paulo Freire as one of my fathers, or one of my brothers. I inherited his work; *we* who try to link writing and freedom projects inherited his work, collectively.

Q. Since as you point out all scientific narratives are in contestation for acceptance and thus dominance, can we really avoid this same struggle between traditional narratives and those deriving from standpoints of situated knowledge?

A. No, we can't. The call for a truly new story is a kind of conventional, generic, ecstatic move, a kind of slogan work, and so one would hate to be held to that way of phrasing one's project in some sort of comprehensive way; but it's a statement of desire, a kind of yearning for something that's new, a kind of yearning for the relief of suffering in fairly traditional terms. It's the attempt (and I think I get this from literary practice, but "literary" in the broad sense) to re-narrate, to produce women's writing, to produce a female symbolic where the practice of making meanings is in relationship to each other, where you're not simply inheriting the name of the father again and again and again. So part of the freedom projects among communities that have found themselves in positions of the dominated (which is never absolutely) is that yearning for systems of reference, systems of civilization, figuration, narration that are in relation to each other. You reconstruct inheritance. There's a really fine writer, Vicki Smith, a new faculty member in English at Miami University, who's talking about the re-narration of loss and dereliction in women's stories as the mechanism for producing a female symbolic.

Perhaps we can transport that into areas of science and technology. I feel very strongly that technoscience is inherently narrative. That's not all it is, but it is inextricably about building stories into the world, building ways of life, building stories and situating subjects in these stories; living within technoscience is living a story. Reconfiguring the terms of that story—who are the actors, what are the plot structures, what kinds of action can be included in that story, how many layers of meanings are allowed to show— is what I mean by building new stories. The traditional narratives of science and technology divide the technical from the political, divide scientists from some peculiar ontological thing called "the public," and then the public gets tested on whether it understands or not: do they know what the ozone hole is, what does the public think about *X*, are scientists misunderstood? You get a whole set of very traditional divisions between the technical and the political. The main commitment I have is to re-fuse the technical and the political in a non-trivial way that is also not relativist. When you re-fuse the technical and the political, you insist on the story-ladenness of knowledge, the story-ladenness of facts. You're not thereby saying, "anything goes," or "it's just what you think," or "it's simply that you have the power to enforce your point of view." It's not a cynical or a relativist position, but it is about the materiality of anything that's going to be able to count as knowledge; it's about the irreducible historical specificity and materiality of these matters, which I think is the opposite of relativist.

Q. Are there any misunderstandings of your work that you'd like to address?

A. One of them that just really does gall me is the reading of my work, from the "Cyborg Manifesto" on, as a sort of techno-phillic love affair with techno-hype. A fair number of people (I think in deep bad faith) read me as some blissed-out, cyborg propagandist and really don't want to understand the way that *I* read the cyborg figure. I want to read the cyborg figure as a much more fraught, kind of limited trope that's about the kind of pain as well as possibility involved in contemporary technoscience and the inextricable weave of bodies and machines and meanings. So, it's those who appropriate my work and take quotes out of context and put them into *Wired* magazine or *Mondo 2000* that make me very upset. It's losing control of your own meanings. And then there's a kind of parallel misunderstanding by people who I feel I'm with, often other feminists, who sometimes read my work in the same way but then put a negative value on it. It's very important for me to be in a community of people who have a culture of disagreement and who are working with and against each other without pegging each other like butterflies, without taking some position out of its historical moment and pinning you with it—the kind of thing we often do to each other as a mode of critical discourse.

🐞 🐞 🐞

Sandra Harding

Q. Do you think of yourself as a writer?

A. Yes, I do. My seventh-grade journalism teacher, in the little memory book that your classmates write things in when you're ready to graduate, wrote, "Sandra, you are going to be a great writer." I found it so mysterious: how could this person tell? And for three decades it meant nothing to me. I think precisely because I write to people in different disciplines, I'm very conscious of the *writing*, of not just *speaking* what I'm thinking but very much trying to direct my writing toward one audience or another and of thinking about where readers are coming from. I try to key my writings into literatures that are familiar to the people that I'm writing for—with greater or less success, as the case may be. So, I do think of myself as a writer; it's a very conscious process. But I think that coming from analytic philosophy is a serious obstacle to being a good writer for anybody but analytic philosophers. On the one hand, I'm criticized for my writing: non-philosophers find it dull and turgid. I remember a review in *The Nation* said, "Unfortunately, a major flaw with this book is its turgid writing style." My department chair said, "That guy doesn't read any philosophy." On the other hand, philosophers regard my writing as not philosophical enough: it uses metaphors and does things that analytic philosophers are not supposed to do.

Q. Would you describe your writing process?

A. I usually start with an argument in mind—some view I'm criticizing, not necessarily an individual, but some assumption or some claim—and develop a little paragraph argument. So, the beginning of the process is an outline and a short abstract. I then start writing. There are two things that I discovered are unusual, at least in talking with other people, about how I write (though I'm sure that other people do it too, that I'm not unique). One is that I don't write from beginning to end. I do the outline, then I do little abstracts of the arguments in the different sections, and then I start on whatever I think is the hardest section to write. So, I go from an abstract to an outline to say a six-page version of a forty-page paper, and then I pick whatever's the most problematic aspect— the thing that I can't envision, that is least clear to me—and I try to write that section up into, say, a ten-page version. (I aim for a paper that's at least fifty percent longer than what I'm going to have to end up with.) Then I go back and work with the other sections, kind of growing them up and keeping them in balance with each other, and keeping the outline and the text in some kind of positive relationship to each other. I adjust the outline to the text, and I have to keep the outline there continually or I lose where I am. So, the writing process for me is really a learning process. I don't just compose the whole paper in my head and then write it down, which some people do. Working with the arguments is a learning process. The other thing I do is throw away a lot of first drafts. Sometimes I throw away three drafts of a paper (I did that recently). I toss them and just sit down and start over. I don't look at them and pull things from them.

Well, I don't always throw them away. Sometimes I feel that they're not strong enough, that they're not powerful enough: either they're not addressing the right audience or they're not organized in the right way for that particular audience or they're usually too conservative. Often in the process of working on the first draft and then setting it aside for some period of time (at least three weeks, maybe longer), I realize that the heart of the paper is not where I thought it was, that it's boring or too hard to do, that it's somewhere else. And so I just set it aside. My computer directory is full of these different versions of the paper, and later I may go and take a paragraph or a section out of one after I've got the second paper well formulated. But I start with the second paper in the same way that I did the first paper. . . .

We can't control the ideas and movements we set in motion. I often feel that way about my own writing, my own books: they're like children that you send out into the world, and you wouldn't believe what they do out there. Then I try to get them back, straighten them out, shape them up, and send them out there again. I feel that my own texts continually have to be struggled for; each time one's read, it's a different text that is read, and it's a new book that's out there. I do believe that its meaning is constructed by readers. You saw me smiling at some of the strange rhetoric I was using ten years ago; it sounds very different to me now than it did then.

Q. Given recent intellectual trends toward dissolving disciplinary borders, how do you guard against the *mis*appropriation of the scholarship of one field by the scholars of another?

A. For me this isn't an issue about dissolving disciplinary borders, though I understand how disciplinarians could perceive it that way. It's rather an issue about having conversations across, from inside to outside, disciplinary borders. Let me be concrete. Scientists always talk outside science: they're always in Congress, on television, and down the hall being interviewed by *Newsweek*. It's not that they talk only to themselves; it's that they claim expertise about nature and about the nature of science. Philosophers do the same thing, so it's not peculiar to science; every discipline does it. We think that we're the experts about our own particular field. What else were we in college for all those years? Why else are we hired by these departments if we're not experts about our own particular field? I don't think you can guard against the misappropriation of scholarship of one field by the scholars of another. Cross-field appropriation is a crucial element in how knowledge advances; taking models, methods, metaphors, and ways of thinking from one field and applying them to another is exactly the way science progresses. Kuhn has a discussion of this, about how paradigm shifts are not generated by people *in* the field because they're too socialized into the field, too invested in the older ways of doing things. Such shifts tend to come about by people who are well trained in some discipline or another, so that they know what it is to be disciplined, to be a rigorous thinker; but because their thinking has not been constrained by that field, they're able to think new thoughts about that field and to ask new kinds of questions. What is a misappropriation? Is it taking my work and using it in ways I didn't intend? In literary studies they talk about the death of the author; I think we should talk about the death of the scientist in the very same way: scientists can't—in fact, don't—control how their work is used. In one way they understand this; they always say, "We have no responsibility for our work once it leaves our laboratories." In another way, they claim that their intentions are what constrains the way anybody can read their theories: if they didn't intend evil, then there is no evil that comes out of their theories; it comes from somewhere else. This is not helpful. So, what is a misappropriation of scholarship? I'm not arguing that there aren't misunderstandings and unfortunate uses of theories from one field to another—there are. But these are the very same processes that also result in very creative uses of work from another field. The way one not *guards* but *works* against non-useful appropriations of work from one field to another is by arguing against them. If we think that biological determinism is not useful for understanding social phenomena, then we need to argue against it, to provide evidence and show how models that work with termites may explain a great deal but may not be the best models for explaining the French Revolution, the American Revolution, or the writing of *Sociobiology*, that very book itself. We need to make the arguments themselves. That's probably the kind of thing someone would think is a misappropriation of one field to another.

❦ ❦ ❦

bell hooks

Q. Do you see yourself as a writer, an author?

A. I do. I think I now see myself more as a writer because it has become so evident that I have an audience, because I now get so much feedback. I found it hard to think of myself as a writer when I felt I was writing in isolation with no clear sense of an audience because for me writing as a writer implied mutuality, that there is both reader and writer.

Q. So the audience made you a writer.

A. Absolutely. I feel that really strongly. Each year of my life, I feel I'm writing with a deeper dedication because it's so clear that the audience grows stronger.

Q. What's your writing process like?

A. Well, one dreary thing that I do is handwrite everything; I've handwritten all my books. I like to handwrite because I find that I think differently when I do so. Computers are seductive in that you feel that you don't have to edit and rework as much because the printed text can look so good, and if you have a good printer it looks even better. So for me the stages tend to be that I work something through in my head, and then I start writing it. And I work a lot with question outlines because the question-and-answer format is one I like a lot and use often in writing essays. I think: "What kind of questions do I envision myself and another audience wanting to know, say, about this film or about this issue?"

Also, I keep a journal, and I write in it every day to try to get a handle on why I'm doing something or what I hope to accomplish by doing it. Asking such hard questions of ourselves usually compels us to hone our perspective.

Q. You experiment with various alternatives to traditional academic prose, including interviews, self-interviews, and dialogues. Do you see such forms as ways to resist traditional, patriarchal discourse?

A. Oh, absolutely! I think one of the primary reasons for using these forms is a lesson I learned from the Shahrazad Ali book. When I saw all those poor underclass and lower-middle class people on the subways of New York and in bus stations reading that book, I wondered, "What's so magical about this book? It's not just the content." What I realized was that you could open that book to any page, and any paragraph would make sense; it shared an idea with you. And I realized that conversation books are like that. One of the things I've been thinking a lot about is that I find that lately I read less. I used to pride myself on reading a book a day, because reading was a passion for me. But now I'm lucky if I read a book a week. In busy times I'm lucky if I read a book in two weeks. I wondered how we expect people who work every day to come home and read these ten- and twenty-page essays we are taught to write in the academy. And so I learned from Shahrazad Ali that you can write a kind of book like *Breaking Bread* (which is the conversational book) in which people can come home and open it up to any page and read that page and feel that they got some idea and that they understood it, that they could digest it. Then I got a lot of feedback from readers who said, "I found I could come home from work, open up *Breaking Bread*, and just read maybe a couple of pages." This is a real challenge to us as academics who have been trained to write longer pieces, and I see it as a subversion of the whole sense that there has to be only one monolithic writing style that can be given scholarly legitimation in the academy. Sometimes I write ten pages of something and I think this could have just as well been said in three pages, but most journals aren't going to want to publish three pages. I'd like to see journals become more open to publishing smaller pieces if we can truly say what we have to say in that short space.

Q. In what way is the personal potentially an important component of scholarly writing?

A. If you look at my first two books, you see very little personal anecdote, personal confession. What I began to find was that when you're trying to invite people to shift their paradigms more pragmatically or concretely—for example, I'm trying to get black people to think about feminism and often there's resistance— usually if you just start off from the purely theoretical or the abstract (and I don't think theory and abstraction are one and the same), people don't tend to open up if they already have that resistance. We had a good example of it in a talk I gave today. A young black brother said, "I came here not knowing your work, assuming that you were anti-black-male." If I had not told the kinds of anecdotes that showed my regard for black males, my concern for their well being, I don't think he would have opened up. This is something that has made me think a lot about the personal story as a teaching tool. I gave a lecture recently at the MMLA, and I talked about my concern about everything being personalized. Someone stood up in the question-and-answer period and said that he was sorry to hear me say this because so much of my work has been personal. I replied, "I don't think of *personal* and *personalize* as the same thing. For me, *personalize* means that you see everything as coming back to your ego and to your narcissistic construction of self." I said that I saw my willingness to be more confessional about my life and to share experiences as part of a kind of activism that is about sacrifice for me. I also said that I'd like to spend a year of my life when maybe I *wasn't* sharing in a public arena details of my personal life, but I have found those details often to be what grabs people, and it's what makes theory seem (as it does for me) to have concrete application. When you tell a story about how you use an abstract idea or a bit of theory in a concrete situation, it just feels more real to people.

Q. Do you believe writers should "ignore" audience, that awareness of audience can be a *disabling* concern, or do you think writers should develop an ever sharper sense of audience?

A. We need to do both. I've just finished writing a piece on censorship. I was struck by the fact that I was very disturbed by Henry Louis Gates' op-ed piece on anti-semitism in the *New York Times*, and I wanted to write a response, but I felt that I shouldn't, that it was inappropriate, that I would be perceived as attacking a black man, and so I thought to myself that I shouldn't write this piece. I thought about other academics who would say I'm trashing Skip, and I was worried that Skip would see me as not supporting him. That's the kind of case where too much recognition of audience can be dangerous. This is a very dangerous phenomenon in academe right now. When intellectuals constitute a rising social class—and I think we see a rising sort of clique in a sense with some black intellectuals—then there's a kind of censorship that says, "Well, maybe I should go out and have a drink with this person and tell him what I don't like about his essay, but I shouldn't write a public response." I really grappled with this question. I said, "My God, if I who have tenure and a clear sense of where I'm going feel that I can't write a critique for fear of how other people might respond, then what must someone who has no job security, who has to fear that this powerful black male academic might have a say in their future, feel?" It stunned me just how dangerous that kind of climate is. In that sense, thinking too much about audience can be dangerous. Yet, thinking about audience can be crucial for marginalized people who haven't had voice but who are trying to come to grips with a voice. In a sense, when I was eighteen and nineteen and was writing the first draft of *Ain't I a Woman*, I had a very artificial academic voice. *Ain't I a Woman* didn't get published until six years or so after I wrote it, and it initially had a lot of stilted language. When I began to imagine myself speaking to other black women, I was able to break out of the jargon that I had learned as the appropriate academic tone. I think that was a way in which thinking of audience was positive and constructive. Sometimes it's good to think about the audience you want to reach because we can reach different audiences in different ways.

Q. One audience you have *not* catered to is the traditional literary-critical establishment.

A. We've seen a great welling up of literary criticism about African American texts. To me, an interesting question is to what extent does literary criticism help create a critical readership? Part of what has made me distance myself from writing literary criticism as much as I write other things is that literary criticism doesn't participate as much as I would like it to in creating a critical readership, in educating people for critical consciousness. That may have had more to do with the *type* of literary criticism we've been writing, but I have not nurtured that aspect of my intellectuality as much because of the fact that so few people read it. Once you have a book that five-thousand people have read (which doesn't seem like a lot, but for academics that's a lot of readers), to think that you will labor over an essay that only ten people might read is really hard. What's great is when we have the luxury of the option to do both. I would never feel happy just to have that limited readership; at the same time, it's also okay when people want to write something that may only be magic for a small audience. I don't want to denigrate that. I think we can have both. It was interesting that at the end of a public lecture I gave today, quite a number of people came up to say that they had, in fact, read the lit-crit articles I've done on Hurston and Walker and which were published in more obscure places and don't have much accessibility. This showed me that people do read those things, but rarely do people write to me about those pieces. It's the whole question of to what extent people feel they can use critical work, critical thinking, in their lives. And I think that cultural criticism seems to excite so many of us right now precisely because it seems to make students think, "Wow! there really is something to theory and to thinking about this stuff that I can translate back to my lived reality." Once you're seduced by the potentiality of a larger audience and a larger critical dialogue, it's hard to engage in certain forms of writing that close down the possibility of larger audiences.

Q. You say in *Breaking Bread*, "When I look at the evolution of my identity as a writer I see it intimately tied to my spiritual evolution."

A. I believe I was thinking about the question of contemplation. A lot of people ask me, "How do you write all these books?" I used to joke, "Oh, it's because I don't have a life." But I think the real answer is that I spend a lot of time alone, and I believe that the act of writing isn't just about spending the time alone writing; it's also the time you spend in contemplation. My development as an intellectual and as a critical thinker is tied to spirituality because growing up as a working-class black woman, the only arena of my life that gave me the sense that I had the right to a space of contemplation was religiosity and spirituality. In fact, it was telling me that everybody needs to go into the desert and to be alone. Given the kind of racist, sexist iconography in our culture that always presumes that black women should serve the interests of others, whether it's black children or black men or the larger society, it's very hard for black women to claim that space that is the precursor to writing, the space where you can think through ideas. This is a way in which those two experiences of spiritual practice and writing converge for me. Also, I'm really engaged with Buddhism. I just did a big interview in *Tricycle*, a marvelous, new Buddhist magazine that covers various cultural issues and tries to relate Buddhist practice in the United States to other aspects of our culture. One of the things I like about Buddhism is its emphasis on practice; when I apply that to writing, writing becomes a form of practice that gives me the energy to spend long hours. I just finished a long piece on Jean-Michel Basquiat, the twenty-seven-year-old black painter who has a retrospective at the Whitney right now. I meditated a great deal because I felt that there was kind of a white supremacist art hegemony that was writing very negative cultural criticism about his work and art criticism. I felt that I really wanted to be able to write something that would illuminate the beauty and power I find in his work. I thought about it, I read a lot of things, and then all of a sudden after months and months that "rush" came. I sat for hours at the computer—I mean serious, say, ten-hour periods. I have evolved into someone who sits in meditation and who values that kind of immersion. When I finished this piece, I felt ecstasy, the ecstasy of being able to make an intervention. I felt that the piece had a lot of power. I called it "Altars of Sacrifice: Remembering Basquiat," alluding to a black church song: "You're all on the altar of sacrifice laid." Again, it's that convergence for me of motifs of spirituality and cultural criticism.

❦ ❦ ❦

Luce Irigaray

Q. Do you consider yourself a writer?

A. How do you believe I could respond to you? Please note that
you've put "writer" (*un écrivain*) in the masculine, but let that
pass. I don't know if it's a problem of translation. What is a
writer for you, in the first place? And in the second place, is it
really up to me to decide if I'm a writer or not? I'm astonished
to think that someone is able to decide for herself if she is a
writer or not.

   I want to make a comment useful for you and, I think, for many
American readers and especially for many feminist readers, male
and female, worldwide. I think that in the United States my books
are read mainly in literature departments. But they are philosophical books and I think that there is a great deal of misunderstanding
about them because the heart of my argument is philosophical,
and literary scholars are not always prepared to understand this
philosophical core. Along these lines, I want to say that the
questions you pose are tied to your literary training and that the
audience, moreover, is literary. These are questions that speak
only to certain aspects of my work. Perhaps it's not pleasing that
I say this, but at the same time I think it's useful. To make a work
rigorous, it's necessary to agree on what's at stake in the work,
and, even more, to agree that I speak as a woman and that the thing
most refused to a woman is to do philosophy. It's always been
admitted that women are able to create literature—at least a little,
if they have time—but philosophy, by means of which values are
defined, that was strictly reserved for men.

Q. Is your work truly translatable?

A. If my work—now, notice how I've put this—if my work represents difficulties of translation, I'd say these are above all difficulties of syntax, logical difficulties, more than phonetic ones. I also

think that there are two aspects of the problem of translation. The first thing that I've already spoken about is that very few male or female translators really read me as a philosopher and thus make interpretive errors about my text because of this problem. Also, errors of translation may come from the fact that I am opening a new field of thought. For example, there's a central part of *Speculum* that's called "L'incontournable volume." The American woman who translated it entitled this chapter "Volume Fluidity." In the anthology published by Blackwell, the chapter is retranslated because the people at Blackwell and Margaret Whitford retranslated it, but there are new errors in their translation. My attention was drawn to the Italian translation made by someone competent, a [female] philosopher, but for whom my thought was, more or less, something completely new, at least then. But in Italian, in any case, the term "incontornabile" exists. By "L'incontournable volume" I simply meant a volume that can't be circumscribed because it's open. Thus, it didn't mean either "volume fluidity" or "volume without contours." It's an allusion to the morphology of the female body, and I say that this morphology is an open volume, one that can't be circumscribed. A closed volume can be circumscribed; an open volume can't be circumscribed. Why do people make this mistake? Because they fail to listen and lack the imagination that corresponds to what I mean.

I want to give another example since you've spoken of translation. *Speculum* has as its subtitle *de l'autre femme*, and it's true that I was imprudent [in so titling it]. With this title and subtitle I meant two things. Almost everybody understood the term "speculum" as simply the term "mirror." But the title evokes much more than this: it's an allusion to those European works (I'm no longer sure of exactly what era) that speak of the "speculum mundi"—that is, the "mirror of the world." It's not simply a question of a mirror in which one sees oneself, but of the way in which it's possible to give an account of the world within a discourse: a mirror of the world. How I'm going to try to give an account of the world in my discourse. It's in this sense above all that I also played with the mirror, but not simply, because the mirror in a simple sense, in which I see myself, has served for the most part to constitute a masculine subject. And the subtitle was even more striking, because in French it's *de l'autre femme*. Apparently I was imprudent because in *Speculum* I play with words all the time. I should have put after *de l'autre* a colon: *de l'autre: femme* [of the other: woman], meaning the other *as* [*en tant que*] woman. Then in Italian the subtitle became *Speculum*: *L'altra donna* [*Speculum: The other woman*]. Everybody thought it was a question of the image of the other woman—that is, they thought of an empirical relation between two women, for example. This is absolutely not the project of *Speculum*. In American it became *Speculum of the Other Woman*. That's worse, because it should have been put, *Speculum on the Other Woman* or *On the Other: Woman*. That would have been best. It was there, that moment, that marked the counterpoint to Simone de Beauvoir. That is, Simone de Beauvoir refused to be the Other because she refused to be second in Western culture. In order not to be the Other she said, "I want to be the equal of man; I want to be the same as man; finally, I want to be a man. I want to be a masculine subject." And that point of view I find is a very important philosophical and political regression. What I myself say is that there is no true Other in Western culture and that what I want— certainly I don't want to be second—but I want there to be two subjects. Thus, it was "On the Other: Woman." And these are things that have involved an equally great misunderstanding of my work, so that it's been thought that in the second part of my work I turn my back on the first, that I renounce the first part. This error follows, among other things, from errors of translation in the title and subtitle of *Speculum*. I've never been repressive about homosexuality, but in *Speculum* I didn't want to treat a problem between two women. I wanted to treat the problem of the Other as woman in Western culture.

The advice I give to readers is to be bilingual; that's the best. And to read, to read in English and French and compare them. To male and female translators, I would advise that they talk with me about the translation. I think it's very important not to sell texts with errors in them. Also for the translator, because, as there are international translations, one day people will laugh at a poor translation, and meanwhile at the cultural level several years are lost with a bad translation.

Q. As a writer, you've resisted attempts to divide up your work according to the law of genre into fictional and nonfictional, philosophical or poetic, essayistic and analytic texts. Why is this important to you?

A. I recognize the point of this question, although I'm now at another stage, but I'll respond because it's a question for literary people, or at the frontier between literature and philosophy. In the first place, I want to say that I resist genres because in Western tradition to pigeon-hole onself in a genre is to accept a hierarchy—let's say, between philosophy first and then art—and thus to accept that the artistic subject is second in relation to the subject who defines truth first. This I don't want. I resist perhaps because I'm a woman, and traditionally women have always had a way of speaking, of expressing themselves artistically rather than sim- ply, coolly, logically, and I don't want to participate in the repression of this mode of expression. Neither do I want to remain within literature. I'd like to say also that I resist genres because, and above all, what matters to me is opening new ways of thought. That is, I want to think and I don't want simply to submit myself to the traditional categories of logic and understanding, not simply. To accede to these new ways of thought, it's necessary to find a new mode of thinking, a new mode of speaking. I'm not the first to say so; for example, Nietzsche said so, Heidegger said so. I think it's extremely important to accede to thinking and not remain within the logical categories of an intelligence of commentary, or an intelligence of abstract rationality. I want to find a way of thinking that's been forgotten in Western tradition.

Q. Would you comment on the way your books were composed as volumes?

A. *Speculum* isn't merely tripartite. It's a book written in three parts, but it's also necessary to emphasize that the parts are historically inverted. That is to say, it begins with Freud and ends with Plato, and there is a redoubling in the very interior of the book; thus, the book is called *Speculum* and the central part is called "Speculum." There is throughout a play of historical reversals and of doubles that is much more than tripartite. Accordingly, the middle of the book is called "L'incontournable volume"—that is, the volume that can't be circumscribed. *Ethique* is a book that's much less composed; it simply follows the historical order of my seminars. *Elemental Passions* is composed directly, yes. Since you ask, "How were these volumes composed?" I will restrict my comment to three words—how can I say them? I can say first, I hope, *artistically*. That is, for me a book is also an art object; thus I compose my book and I'm not at all content to have an editor change my composition. In general, I refuse changes. For example, when I received the proofs to *Marine Lover of Friedrich Nietzsche* all the blanks had been suppressed and I had to recompose the whole thing. Thus, I would say first, "artistically." At the philosophical level, I'd say there is in my composition a counterpoint between—this is difficult, it's important to find just the right words, otherwise they're going to make errors—between that which concerns the order of schematism and that which concerns the order of discourse. And I would say thirdly, I compose my books as if I were able to speak silently; that is, I always create a counterpoint between speech [*la parole*] and silence.

Q. In "The Three Genres" you characterize "style" in language as "that which resists formalization." Do you accept the identification of "style" with the feminine? How can a writer cultivate her style? And finally, what's the importance of style in your own writing practice?

A. I would like to note that most of the questions concern a meta-discourse of Luce Irigaray (above all don't say Irigaray; I have a horror of that). In other words, you always ask me to take a reflexive, critical position on my work, which corresponds to one of the things I want to avoid. [Laughs.] I can do it, but I'm afraid interviews of this type can undo the effect of the way in which I write. It's for this reason too that at a certain moment I don't want to offer commentary; I want to give some beacons, but no more. Above all, translate my words literally. For example, when I speak of "schematism" I'm alluding to Kant's word. If you use some other word, what I said no longer makes sense.

To continue to respond to your question: I want to say that in our tradition we are submitted to a type of logical formalization. When I don't use a flat pronouncement to explain myself, I cross the formalization of writing with logical formalization. This is what makes my utterance [*parole*] place itself at the crossroads of a double *mise en forme*. And that permits, first, the production of new meaning effects and, above all, leaves the text always open [*entre-ouvert*]—in that it's not enclosed within either a logical formalization or a literary formalization. It's at the encounter of the two. Thus, the text is always open onto a new sense, and onto a future sense, and I would say also onto a potential "You" [*Tu*], a potential interlocutor. That's what I'm able to say.

You ask, "Do you accept the idea that style is feminine?" I'm going to respond in a way that's deliberately rather lapidary and for some people provocative. If you think that the feminine is diverse, as I believe, because subjectivity is diverse, then evidently style is diverse—short of its being a pure and simple technology. But then I don't know if it's possible to talk about a concrete subject, a feminine subject.

As to how a writer can develop her style, I'd respond much the same way. Firstly, I don't think it's possible to have generalizations, and it displeases me to issue a norm for others, but I'd say that thought seems to me to permit the deployment of art, not only thought but also art, because it permits an escape from imitation. Most people who write or paint have begun with imitation. I think that if one permits it, thought will liberate itself from imitation and create its own way. And that also permits its own liberation from the status of pure and simple technique.

Q. One striking feature of your own writing practice is the use of interrogatives to produce a wide range of effects. Would you comment on this aspect of your "style"?

A. I think the importance of the interrogative is to leave a place for the future, thus not to establish a truth that would be a truth once and for all, and also to leave a place for the other—to leave a place for a way toward that other or for the other toward me. I think that's the best explanation of the interrogative. Interrogation is a very good means of passage because the way is always open.

Q. You have argued that it's essential for women to accede to the place of the "I" and you also call for "the transformation of the autobiographical 'I' into a different cultural 'I'." But in "A Chance for Life" you also urge women "never [to] give up subjective experience as an element of knowledge." How do these concerns relate to the role of the "I" in your own writings? Does your theorizing draw upon your own "subjective experience" as a woman?

A. I think that in these questions and in what you proffer as a possible contradiction on my part there is manifest something that for me is a certain impasse of subjectivity. No, I mean a certain way of feminine subjectivity expressing itself, at least that which she's been permitted historically, and that which risks becoming a certain impasse in the liberation of women. Then, many women have understood (no doubt because they needed to), that liberation for them was simply to say "I." They've begun to say "I" and have become a bit lost in this "I" because this "I" lacks, as the philosophers say, categories. Or then they fight among themselves to see who says "I" the loudest: your "I" versus my "I." Certainly, it was important to begin to venture to take the word and venture to say "I," but what seems more important to me, and in any case indispensible to the stage we're now at, is to say not only "I" but to say "I-she" (*Je-elle*)—that is, to live that "I" and define it not only as a simple subjectivity that expresses itself, but in terms of a dialectic between subjectivity and objectivity. Then, I myself write "I" as "I marked she" (*Je indice elle*), which permits me to make visible that the subject is two, that it's not a unique subject, and to pose all sorts of dialogic questions. For example, what is a dialogue between "I-she" and "You-she," a dialogue between "I-she" and "You-he," a dialogue between "I-he" and "You-she"? All these kinds of questions, the dialogic intersection between two differently adhering subjects, two generically different subjects, become possible.

Thus, if you like, I think that the purely narrative, autobiographical "I," or the "I" that expresses only affect, risks being an "I" that collapses back into a role traditionally granted to woman: an "I" of pathos, that the woman also uses in her place, the home. It seems to me important to accede to a different cultural "I"—that is, to construct a new objectivity that corresponds not to an indifferent "I" but to an "I" that's sexed feminine. It's necessary to remain both objective and subjective. And to remain within a dialectic between the two. I think the way I use the "I" is different depending on each text. The way of using "I" at one moment of my work is to refuse to pretend to dictate truth for others; that is, it's a certain strategy for breaking with a traditional philosophical subject and one that parenthesizes the fact that it's "he" who dictates the truth. In other words, I, Luce Irigaray, at this moment in history; I think there's a humility and a singularity at the philosophical level. At certain times, I think there's a dialectical strategy, but especially in the most recent books; for example, in *Essere Due* there are many dialectical strategies already in the title but also in the interior of the text, where I try to define what could be a double utterance [*une parole à deux*] that would respect the

"I" and the "You" [*Tu*]. Thus, I use the "I" also to indicate speech [*le discours*]. The fact is I can't offer a single explanation that would apply to the collection of my works.

Yes, I draw on my personal experience if that means that I don't write or think in a purely abstract and insensible fashion. The truth I talk about is a truth that's also a sensible truth, one that changes with experience. The experience may be more immediately perceptual or more spiritual. I can say that, and I can also say that I don't think simply in order to depart from the thinking of others. Thus, yes, it goes by way of my personal experience—but I don't want you to put it that way, because it's very complicated. I can't myself, all alone, affirm my own experience, since this is something I know only after the fact, by means of discussion, and so on. I can't affirm that this is always already the experience of a woman. It must be a dialectic between subjectivity and objectivity.

Q. Are you aware of any misreadings or misunderstandings of your work that you'd like to address here?

A. There are certainly errors of translation; I've given you examples. There are errors of interpretation which are tied to something I've already indicated: the principal points of error derive from not being sufficiently attentive to my philosophical training, and especially to my relationship to ontology and to the negative. In the same vein, errors result from confusing a scientific with a philosophical discipline, which aren't the same thing. Obviously, I represent a snare for the reader to the extent that I have various scientific trainings—linguistic, psychological, psychoanalytic, literary (my first studies were literary)—and at the same time, a philosophical training. So I make use of scientific techniques; sometimes I make an analysis of discourse using only a scientific technique. Fundamentally, what I recur to the most in interpretation is, I think finally, a certain philosophical level. So when I'm read simply as a psychoanalyst or as a linguist, there are some

levels of thought, intention, and interpretation in my work that are
already lost.

There is also another error. I think Simone de Beauvoir said
that woman remains always within the dimension of immanence
and that she's incapable of transcendence. But—by I don't know
what mystery!—transcendence is something that interests me
very much. Often the way in which I'm read and interpreted is too
immanent, too much tied to contiguity, and the source and
reference of my work is misunderstood. It's true that a woman
who has a relationship to transcendence and to the transcendental
in a real rather than a formal way is something all too rare. But I'd
say there's been a little of that in my life.

Another error occurs when filiations are imputed to me that are
not mine: for example, it's said that I'm a daughter of Simone de
Beauvoir and that I haven't acknowledged enough the source of
my thinking in relation to her. But that's because I'm not a
daughter of Simone de Beauvoir. I don't know her work well. I
read her novels when I was an adolescent. Two years ago I tried,
for the sake of my students, to take another look at *The Second Sex*;
in fact, I read it in 1952 and read only the Introduction and a little
of the first chapter, but this is not at all the source of my work. And
I've even commented recently about the time when *Speculum*
came out and I sent it to Simone de Beauvoir, and I was very
disappointed when she didn't respond to me—very disappointed,
especially because I had much trouble on account of *Speculum*. I
was excluded from the university, and afterward in France I
couldn't get a teaching appointment. I still don't have one. So I'm
not a daughter of Simone de Beauvoir; I think my theoretical
filiation, as I've always said (it's in all my books), is much more
to the tradition of Western philosophy. Now, I'm not saying that
Simone de Beauvoir isn't part of that tradition, but hers isn't an
oeuvre that I know well nor to which I myself especially refer. It's
possible that I've been influenced by her work by means of the
ideological climate, but I'm not someone who lives very much
in that world. Once again, the question of the Other as she
treats it, and the question of the Other as I treat it, as I was just

saying, are radically different. She refuses to be Other and I demand to be radically Other in order to exit from a horizon. I think they even say I'm a disciple of Rousseau. I don't know Rousseau's oeuvre well. It's true that when Rousseau's work is explained to me there are certain things that are somewhat similar, but if I'd read much Rousseau I would have said so. I know well the philosophers of whom I speak. Look at my work and you'll see.

❦ ❦ ❦

Ernesto Laclau

Q. Do you think of yourself as a writer?

A. I suppose I can say I am a writer in some sense. The point is that "writing" is not a unified category; it can refer to many different types of writing. I see myself these days as a theoretical writer: the way that I try to operate is basically through the production of theory. That has not always been the case. For instance, when I was in Argentina I worked for several years as the editor of a left-wing weekly, so there I was engaged in some form of journalism.

Q. In Richard Rorty's "liberal utopia," persuasion replaces force as a principal social arrangement. In your critique of Rorty, you demonstrate that not only is it impossible to oppose persuasion and force but that "persuasion is one form of force." You add, however, that persuasion cannot simply be reduced to force. Would you elaborate on the relationship of persuasion, rhetoric, to force?

A. In the first place, the category of persuasion as used by Rorty has played the function of, let's say, reducing the epistemological ambitions of a dialogical exchange. For instance, take the case of Habermas. Habermas maintained that finally a dialogical situation would be able, at least as an ideal point of arrival, to conclude in a situation in which one and only one position is maintained by people engaged in the dialogue. Rorty does not believe that. He believes in the purely conversational nature of the agreement that people reach, and that is why persuasion is a category that is as important for him as it is. Now, what I was trying to do in the piece to which you refer is to deepen this logic of persuasion and to find out whether in persuasion, which is the opposite of force for Rorty, there is not an element of force so that one can deconstruct the opposition persuasion/force. What I think I have shown in that piece is that persuasion, precisely because it never presents an argument that should be accepted algorithmically, involves, if you will, an element of force. For example, if you think of the quasi-logical arguments of Chaim Perelman and his analysis of how persuasion operates, you see that an element of force necessarily has to be included. You persuade by something less than a rational type of demonstration. What is this something less? There you can have many possible answers, and all of them would be valued depending on the situation. For instance, you can provoke the sympathy of the listener. You can, on the other hand, present the argument so forcefully that you intimidate the listener, and you know the whole range of these possibilities.

Now, there is one point that for me is particularly important because it leads to central questions in the theory of hegemony: it is that when you are confronted with a situation in which there is no clear answer but in which an answer is needed nonetheless, the fact that some answer is provided becomes more important than its concrete content. That is an element of force—force not in the sense of physical force, but force in the sense that it is less than purely rational demonstration; purely rational demonstration would absolutely collapse the difference between the *ontic* character of the response and the ontological character of being a response. My argument is that in any dialogical situation these two dimensions never collapse, and that is what leads to the deconstruction of the pure alternative force/persuasion. This concept in another sense—for instance, in the Anglo-American discussion—has been very useful when we come to the notion of decision. A distinction is made between the cause of a decision and the motive of a decision, the cause being what provoked the decision. I think there is nothing more complicated than distinguishing between cause and motive, precisely because a motive is never totally algorithmically grounded. We have to play around the deconstruction of this stark opposition in which traditional rationalistic discourse is grounded.

Q. Some theorists contend that literacy is a key element in the emancipation of oppressed groups. What do you believe is the role of literacy projects in struggles against oppression?

A. As far as I understand the concept, the question of the role of a literacy project conceived in the broad sense would be close to what Foucault called a "proliferation of discourses." In a situation in which emancipatory struggles start, there is always a whole transformation at the discursive level: you know how to handle a set of situations to which you didn't have access before. So discourses against oppression (if we understand by that the notion of literacy in its widest sense) are absolutely essential for any struggle against oppression. And here I would like to add something. In general, situations of oppression are not situations in which the oppressed immediately recognize themselves as such. They are situations in which in some sense the identity of the oppressed breaks up and in which precisely these tools of liberation struggle—discourses—are not present. At the moment in which they start being present, we are in a situation in which oppression begins to be radically a question and in which different outcomes are possible. For example, in many areas of the Third World, you do not find class interests in the classical sense because class interests were conceived as constituted around positions in the production process. What you find in many places in the Third World is that people don't have a precise insertion in the production process because there is a wide situation of social marginality. When you have a situation of social marginality, the idea of an interest given by your objective insertion in the relations of production simply does not work.

I remember, for instance, that in the 1930s in the middle of the world economic crisis, Trotsky wrote that if unemployment were to continue at the present level, we would no longer be able to conceive the unemployed in terms of the Marxian category of an industrial reserve army; and if this were so, the whole Marxian theory of the classes would have to be rethought because the category of classes would not embrace everything that had to be embraced in order to conceptualize oppression. In this situation, you often find that populist discourses emerge. Many times at the level of national politics people start acquiring a sense of identity, and you find that they have to reconstruct at the political level through these discourses (which would be new forms of literacy in the broad sense that we are defining it) an identity which does not emerge spontaneously at the level of civil society. This is why I think there was a shift in my conception about this matter. When Chantal Mouffe and I wrote *Hegemony and Socialist Strategy*, we were still arguing that the moment of the dislocation of social relations, the moment which constitutes the limit of the objectivity of social relations, is given by antagonism. Later on I came to think that this was not enough because constructing a social dislocation—an antagonism—is already a discursive response. You construct the Other who dislocates your identity as an enemy, but there are alternative forms. For instance, people can say that this is the expression of the wrath of God, that this is an expression of our sins and that we have to prepare for the day of atonement. So, there is already a discursive organization in constructing somebody as an enemy which involves a whole technology of power in the mobilization of the oppressed. That is why in *New Reflections* I have insisted on the primary character of dislocation rather than antagonism.

Q. You've said that "There is democracy as long as there is the possibility of unlimited questioning." How do we foster a rhetoric of questioning?

A. Paulo Freire would have good answers to this question, but I'm not really the person to answer it. However, what I would like to elaborate on for a moment is the strong distinction—question and answer. The point is: is there any question that is not already in some sense an answer to what it is posing? I think questions do not operate as purely neutral, leaving the field of the answer entirely open; rather, questions operate in the sense of narrowing the field of the answer. So questioning is already the first step in the organization of a discursive field. If we are speaking about literacy in the wide sense, as in the previous question, in that case, to create a culture of questions is absolutely important and is perhaps what distinguishes a dogmatic education or a dogmatic approach to any kind of social practice from a position that is not dogmatic, that is open. It cannot be totally open because in that case there would be no questions either. But it cannot be entirely closed either. So, I would see the whole complex of the relationship question/answer as a continuum in which there are different levels of closedness. This is important for democratic theory because questions can close a certain field, but they can also constitute a community which poses itself a set of problems while at the same time maintaining relatively open the fields of the answers. A community in which there is no community of questions is not a community at all.

Q. What do you see as the role of the concept of articulation for a theory of writing?

A. Articulation is a category that started being important for this type of analysis only with Althusserianism. Before that we had only heard of articulated lorries. It became a theoretically relevant question precisely because Althusser was trying to think a combination of elements that according to classical Marxist theory were uncombinable because they belong to different stages of social evolution. For instance, the notion of the articulation of the modes of production became very much in use in the 1960s in order to define situations in the Third World where you have an incorporation into a world economy of modes of production which were not capitalist and which, however, were integrated within the structure of world capitalism. The way I have developed the notion of articulation in relation to hegemony is the following: as you very well point out here, we cannot conceive of articulation as the linkage of similar and fully constituted elements, precisely because if the elements were fully constituted, the articulation would not play any kind of a grounding role. If you want to conceive of articulation, you can go for instance to the Saussurian model. In the Saussurian model, as far as language is a system of difference, this means, on the one hand, that the social totality in some sense is presupposed by the signifying totality, let's say. The signifying totality is presupposed by any single act of signification but at the same time is exposed to new elements because new elements are going to produce a new articulation of everything that was within the structure. So, articulation in this sense became the basic category of social analysis as far as all social practices are signifying practices. When I say that I take the best fragments of Marxist theory, what I'm saying is that by these fragments' entering into articulatory practices with other elements, they are transforming their nature. There is a set of categories that still can be there but which, however, play a completely different role than they play in classical Marxism. Now, when you ask me about the concept of articulation in a theory of writing, what are you aiming at?

Q. Can the concept of articulation be used in teaching students to think through writing, to think in the process of writing?

A. I wonder if the most relevant concept for that purpose would not be inscription. That is, any writing is a process of inscription. By "inscription" I mean a process in which through putting two things together, the nature of these two things is in some way modified. For instance, I have long experience as a Ph.D. supervisor. One of the most difficult problems that I have found is that students sometimes establish a radical separation between case study and theoretical framework. With such separation you are in a situation in which the theoretical chapter could be identical in all the dissertations and the case study is the only thing that changes from one to the other, which means that the two things have not been articulated at all. Coming back to the Saussurian example that I was giving before, if language is by definition a system of difference and by extension any signifying structure is like that, then the incorporation of new elements has to modify all the elements of the whole. In theoretical discourses, this means that there is no case study which should not modify the theory as well. If articulation is defined in this sense, the conclusion is that through each case study—in fact, the ideology of the case study has to be broken—the theory itself has to be in some sense modified, modified not in the sense of putting it outside, but modified simply in showing theoretical aspects through a new light; and at the same time, the case study (which is comparatively more easy) can be inscribed within a theory. The moment of inscription operates in two ways. My experience is that this is one of the most difficult things for graduate students to learn how to do. But it makes the whole difference between a purely scholarly exercise—scholarly in the bad sense of the term, of simply showing that you have understood a theory in an effort to be able to competently apply it to some case—and to enter into a process in which the theory illuminates the case and the case illuminates the theory. I think that the whole distinction between empirical and theoretical research has to be put, from this point of view, into question. And from this point of view, the category of articulation can help us think about the matter.

Q. Your work on hegemony suggests that it is *urgent* for critical intellectuals to understand the logic of hegemony and develop our own hegemonic strategies.

A. I see the development of a theory of hegemony as a precondition for any kind of strategic thinking, having to combine various tasks, all of which would involve the expansion of rhetoric and rhetorical argumentation. In the first place, I see that we need to have some sort of combination of what I would call various branches, various kinds of poststructuralist theory—and not only poststructuralism; for instance, the Wittgensteinian approach is very important to this matter. Deconstruction provides us with a discourse concerning the deepening of the logic of undecidability, which, for the reasons I mentioned earlier, becomes central. Lacanian theory provides us with a logic of the lack, the logic of the signifier, which is also a discourse of enormous importance. I am very much against attempts of simply opposing deconstruction to Lacanian theory. The two can be productively combined in a variety of ways. And I think that the whole conception of a microphysics of power can be complementary to this effort. One should not dismiss the work of Foucault (or, for the matter, of Deleuze and Guattari) too easily, as some people tend to do. So what we have is a very complicated discourse that has to combine traditions of thought that began from very different starting points but that are all converging on political analysis. And the analysis of the complexity of present day society has to go together with an analysis of the proliferation of the places of enunciation. For instance, if a study in terms of places of enunciation were made, we would see that the transformation of politics over the last thirty or forty or fifty years—let's say, since the end of the Second World War—has multiplied the places from which politically consequential enunciation is possible. This is linked, at the same time, to the disintegration of classical forms of social aggregation.

Once you have this multiplication of the places of enunciation, you also have a proliferation of rhetorical devices; given that we are dealing with a process of argumentation and that this process of argumentation has to operate at a plurality of levels, we are in a situation in which social theory has to advance in the direction of generalized rhetorics. This means, also, that thought has to be more strategic; it has to emphasize the strategic dimension to some extent (but only to some extent) at the expense of the structural dimensions. A structural analysis tries to define matrixes of the constitution of all possible variations of meaning, while strategic thought tries to see constant displacements of meaning in a regulated way, but the very regulation is something that is submitted to the very process of a displacement. So, this is to some extent the kind of theoretical activity toward which the possibility of formulating a theory of politics oriented in a radical sense has to move.

Q. How do we effect such a monumental conceptual change in people's thinking about freedom?

A. Writing, giving talks. Academics are also part of the real world and their influence should not be undervalued. There are many intermediate areas—some forms of journalism, some other forms of the circulation of ideas—in which it is important to engage oneself. Also, intellectual developments themselves have produced a set of historical effects—the development of Milton Friedman's theory, for example—without which the history of the last few years would have been different. Thatcherism, for example, would not have developed the way it did. I think it is important that intellectuals not only produce high theory but that they also write in ways that are accessible to a wider public. It's very important to develop this intermediate area of discourse. In fact, many people are writing in these ways. This is not to say that abstract theory doesn't have its own role to play, but it's not the only kind of discourse to which we have to devote our time.

❦ ❦ ❦

Jean-François Lyotard

Q. In *Peregrinations* you describe how at the age of fourteen you "began to write poems, essays, short stories, and, later still, a novel" but immediately gave up writing after "the only woman in whom I had confidence decided I was not a true writer." Do you now consider yourself a writer?

A. No, I don't consider myself a writer. That's a good question though because I'm trying to find the appropriate term for the way I write in the general sense. A writer is somebody like Claude Simon or Beckett. *They* are writers. That's to say, they are progressing in a space, a field (but it's not a field) in which they don't know what they have to write. They are confronted with the unknown, and that's to say they are really confronted with language itself. There is a sort of fight, a battle with and against words and sentences and phrases, and that's beautiful and terrible work in a sense, and I admire it. But for my part, I remain a philosopher. Even if sometimes I write in *this* sense—trying to grasp the word to express (I don't like this expression: *express*), to fix a certain word, a certain way of composing a phrase— nevertheless, I still remain a philosopher. That is, I'm guided by meaning, and being guided by meaning means maintaining a certain idea of mastering the material, which is the old philosophical tradition. And it seems to me that this is a poverty and a misery. So, I'm between these two ways of writing. I could say I write in a certain way in which what is implied is necessarily the consciousness of what I have to mean. I could use the term "reflexive writing," though I have no definition of it, but you know what I mean.

Q. In that same book you say that the idea that writing "pretends to be complete," that it presumes to "build a system of total knowledge" about something, "constitutes *par excellence* the sin, the arrogance of the mind." In a postmodern world, how *should* we view the role of writing?

A. In the postmodern world, we have to separate writing as a cultural effect and writing as writing. You can take a book as a cultural object and finally test it as having a large audience or as being understandable—as being a poor work or the opposite, a brilliant one. That's the postmodern appreciation of the works of mind (if I can use this term), of thought, but it seems to me that writing is the opposite: writing is the capacity to resist the network of exchanges in which cultural objects are commodities, and maybe to write is precisely to avoid making a book (or even a small paper or article) a commodity, but rather to oppose, to resist the simple and naive exchangeability of things in our world. That's to say, to write is necessarily to allude to something else which is not easily communicated. It doesn't mean that a work is difficult to read; it could be very simple, but it alludes to something else.

Q. For fifteen years while a member of *Socialisme ou Barbarie*, you gave up all writing except for that devoted to this activist group. You comment that your return to "real (?) writing in the mid-sixties was a sign that my militancy had passed and another mode of legitimation was being searched for." Do you find academic work to be incompatible with social activism?

A. I don't know because I have no experience with academic work. That's true; that's my fate or my destiny, my incapacity. This is so even when I started to write: it was the book called *Discours, figure*, and though it was presented as a dissertation, it wasn't an academic book at all. Even the title was considered bizarre to academic people. I remember two colleagues in the university (it was Nanterre University at that time) looking at the pamphlet announcing the book and saying, "What is this title? It's impossible. This is a dissertation, *Discours, figure*?" In a certain sense, I have no real experience of the academy. I was always a teacher; even now (and I'm at retirement age) I continue for personal reasons to teach, and I like it. In a certain sense, I was very engaged in the direct relationship with young people, with students. But the idea of creating an academic work is not mine because it entails what Lacan called "the discourse of the master," and I'm not about to take myself as a master, just a perpetual student, a child.

My activism was a complete activism. It wasn't simply being a card-carrying member of the party. I was completely engaged twenty-four hours a day because we had to do everything, not only to write but to print, to distribute, to defend, to go to factory entrances in order to distribute pamphlets, to manifest, to make public our meetings in order to propose or to defend our ideas or our analysis about capitalist society and Stalinist society. So it was continual work; it was impossible for me to engage in real academic or even writing activity. When I turned to the book *Discours, figure*, it was a break in my life in a certain sense. Or, rather, this break was what made me capable of having a different life. That is, my writing started, around the middle of the sixties, as the giving up of a political perspective. I realized at that moment that the basis of my political perspective—that is, an alternative to the dominance of capitalist arrangement or organization of things—was impossible, and that there was not another subject, a real and authentic subject. What was called "the proletariat" by Marx didn't exist finally—except as an idea, and the idea was linked to a general metaphysics, the modern metaphysics which makes or made political life in Western countries a sort of tragedy, a battle, a fight between the false subject, capital, and the real one, the proletariat. So, I started to write as a sort of mourning, as a despair, the necessity to come back to these stupid activities because, finally, militant activity was no longer effective.

Q. You suggest that the alternative to the grand Enlightenment narrative of education as emancipation is education as resistance—resistance against the academic genres of discourse, against the great narratives themselves, and "against every object of thought which is given to be grasped through some 'obvious' delimitation, method, or end." How can such resistance be fostered?

A. It's up to each of us. Resistance is not an alternative, properly speaking, in the usual sense of another policy or another politics. It is impossible to base politics on the notion of resistance. It could be very dangerous in that that's the *old* tradition. What was Marxism in the nineteenth century? It was a politics of resistance. Now we know the effects of such politics because it is politics; that's all. A political approach to this problem of resistance is completely wrong. It's impossible to make a front of a resistance party. There is no resistance party because if it is a party, it is no longer resistant; it is a part of the system and in concert with the system. And that's good. I've nothing against it because it is necessary to have at least two parties in order to correct the system itself. Today in all developing societies, that's the general situation: to have two parties in order to balance the correction of arrangements or fitness of the system itself. Maybe we can imagine resistance in terms of the capacity for people (I don't know if it's for all people; I'm not so "rousseauist") to "write" in the sense we used just before: to advance or want something that is not clear, and to discover a means of giving testimony of that which is precisely not yet included in the circulation of commodities; it is not yet known. It seems to me that this is active resistance, not in the sense of a *resistance armée* but in the sense of to wait for, to be passive. It seems to me that the job is to write toward something appealing but to be honorable enough to specify what kind of thing this thing is appealing to—that is, to resist the already done, the already written, the already thought, that's to say precisely commodities, even in the philosophical world or literary field.

Q. You've expressed concern that some of your earlier works, including *The Postmodern Condition*, might appear to privilege narrative over other discursive genres even while it is useful to examine certain "great questions" in historical—that is, *narrative*—terms. You also caution that it is "tempting to lend credence to the great narrative of the decline of great narratives." Do you believe the vocabulary of narratives has outlived its explanatory usefulness and that what is needed is a new vocabulary (in the Rortian sense)?

A. We need new vocabularies all the time, forever. It's a part of the way the system is developing. *It* needs new vocabularies. It's very eager to grasp new vocabularies. Even the resistant work of writers or artists is grasped or memorized by the system because, in short, maybe it can be used. So we need new vocabulary. But as to the question of narrative itself, in my earlier works, yes, I presumably give a sort of privilege to the narrative way of speaking and writing with the sense that that's the basis of any entrance into language. For me, narrative is a childish way, the first way. I have a son who is eight years old (that's already old), and I remember the way in which he grasped information and immediately put it into a small narrative. It's a sort of immediate "composition" (as you would say) of the meaning. Finding the relation between two meaning units is spontaneously a narrative way. And is it possible to overcome? Is it necessary to overcome? No. I think that is very interesting; that's something very mysterious in a certain sense. Take, for example, writers such as James Joyce or even Gertrude Stein or Claude Simon. They are considered to be trying to destroy traditional narratives or a narrative way of writing. That's true in a certain sense; but at the same time, there is a complex, complexified and perverted submission to narrative itself, making narrative *more* important than it is in the traditional fable. It seems to me that there is a resistance of narrative presumably linked with our childhood, with infancy, the space/time during which we were unable to speak but during which we were already capable of having narrative without speaking, if I can say that. (That's my hypothesis, if you'll excuse me.). . . .

Returning to the idea of writing in a general sense and to

resisting by writing, I think that there is a strong relationship, an obscure relationship, between the ability to write in *this* sense and what I could call "femininity" because there is a sort of openness to something unknown without any project to master it, but, rather, the opposite: to work on it. As a male, I represent this attitude as feminine. And I'm sure it's not a job of "composition" (if you'll excuse me), because in composition there is a sort of mastering, of putting things together so as to order them. It seems to me that the opposite is the ability to be weak, a good weakness, so-called passivity. I don't mind this term, though I tried to propose the term *passibility*. In this certain representation we can have the way of thinking in Zen Buddhism or certain Eastern philosophies or religions: the ability to wait for, not to look at, but to wait for—for what, precisely, we don't know. That's my ideological representation of the necessary attitude for writing. When somebody like Flaubert said, "I *am* Madame Bovary," it was not a joke; it was recognizing that he had not only to *be* the character, but to be a *woman* in order to write. The same with Proust. I know a lot of painters—some of them are very great artists—and I recognize their refusal of the temptation to grasp, to master, but the opposite, their acceptance *not* to know as the event they need in order *to paint*. It's an event not to know. It's good; there's no prejudice. That's femininity to me, real femininity. There's presumably unbalanced repetition of this femininity with masculinity in women and men, but I know women who are more male than I am.

Q. In "One Thing at Stake in Women's Struggles," you posit that "the philosopher, as philosopher, is a secret accomplice of the phallocrat" because philosophy is "the search for a constituting order that gives meaning to the world." Certainly you don't mean to suggest that because philosophy "is already the language of masculinity" we should not interrogate gender. How can we escape this problematic and produce useful inquiry about gender and gender relations?

A. Yes, I was right. I think that's very important because finally the phallocratic master is not really capital itself, which is something more complex and perverse. The master was the philosopher in the traditional culture of Western countries, and that's to say, in the term I used, is able "to answer." I ask a question, and reason, the logos, whatever you can imagine, is able to answer. There is something like this in the sciences in the beginning of their history, but now scientists are more timid and prudent in the matter of questions and answers. They are more complex in the way questions are asked and answers can be given to questions. There's sort of a sense now in the sciences that there is perpetual displacement of questions and that answering is never achieved. That's good, and intelligent. But in traditional philosophy this wasn't the case. The people there have the idea that they should build an enormous system of questioning and answering in order to find a system of answers. This is *mastering*, to make language work exclusively for answering, which is a very perverse notion of language. Or even if they were able to answer because they were very intelligent—Plato or Aristotle or even Spinoza—even if they gave a large space to answering a question, the question was asked in the way it had to be answered. That is, the general structure, the form, the start of the use of language was under the edges of this question and its answers. That's the reason I don't like the term *agonistic*. At the end of a lecture is the moment of Q and A. It seems to me dangerous and ridiculous in a certain sense, though necessary. Going back to your question, one of the reasons philosophy properly speaking is in such extreme crisis today (I mean philosophy as a way of discourse) is precisely the fact that certain of the so-called philosophers (maybe Rorty, maybe Davidson, not only the so-called continental philosophers but some of the American philosophers) are asking the question, "Is it right to reduce thinking to a game of questioning and answering with the idea that an answer is possible?" I remember a text by Franz Kafka in which he explains that what is so marvelous is the fact that generally speaking a question is in fact already an answer; it implies in it an answer. A question is not naive; it comes from the previous answer. And what is called "the answer" is only interesting as far as it is a question. That is a good description of what it is to write, as Gertrude Stein has said.

Q. So to produce useful inquiry about gender, then, one should still question but not with the objective of necessarily producing an answer about gender and gender relations?

A. I think that it's impossible. The enormous, extreme, huge importance of the question of gender is precisely that this question has no answer, and that's the only way we can continue to think about it: I try to elaborate, to place femininity and masculinity, but I already know that my answer is a bad one. It's certainly false. It's immediately suspect. And that's good; that's the way we have to approach this question. But this question is enormous; it's a paramount question for somebody who wishes not only to live and to exist but also to think or to write. In a certain sense, you can imagine writing as precisely like how this question of gender is posed and never answered. Maybe that's the best homage we can give to the gender question—to write.

Q. Except for occasional references to Hélène Cixous and Luce Irigaray, you rarely mention the work of the French feminists in your own work. Do you not find French feminist thought useful to your own writing, your own lines of inquiry?

A. Useful, certainly. Cixous must be; *it* must be. In fact, I've known both of them for a long time. I admire certain books written by Hélène. And I had a strong discussion, even dispute, with Luce at an international conference in France at Cerisy. She gave a paper, and I was horrified. The paper was truly feminist, but in a sense I can't accept at all, and we had a strong dispute—a friendly dispute, but strong. Generally speaking, I have good relations with them as persons, but it's true that I've not made real use of their works. I don't know why, frankly. Perhaps it was too late for me, I don't know. I have a stronger relationship with the work of Gertrude Stein. My question to you could be, "Does a feminist woman or man consider Gertrude Stein to be a feminist writer?" This seems to me a real question because in a certain sense I consider some works written by Hélène to be very close to Gertrude Stein's papers or books. It seems to me that the way Gertrude is working through the traditional phrasing of discourse, which is more or less the same way Hélène does, is in a certain sense, properly speaking, feminist—in the sense that we've been talking about. If you open the *Différend* (which is a terrible book, a horrible book), there are "notices" on Kant and Levinas and Plato and Aristotle disseminated throughout the book, and there is a notice on Gertrude Stein—a montage of quotations and two or three questions at the end of this very brief notice. In particular, I asked the question, "Is this what they call feminist writing?" I think it is.

Q. Are there any misunderstandings of your work that you'd care to address at this time?

A. First, one misunderstanding is that some people take me to be a "theorist." I worked in several texts against this idea. I remember in the sixties when structuralist ideology was dominant in France and elsewhere I resisted this way of thinking. It was with a sort of pride (or arrogance) on my part to observe that finally a book like *Discours, figure*—which was completely ignored at the time because it was explicitly against structuralism, not only in terms of linguistic structuralism but even Lacanian structuralism because at that time the Lacanian reading of Freud was similar to Althusser on Marxism—has gained acceptance. I was against this way of thinking, and I am pleased that now readers have discovered this book. I was waiting thirty years—no problem. The point is that I'm not a theorist. Please, don't take the notion of postmodernity as theory. I never used the term *postmodernism*, only "the postmodern" or "postmodernity"—it's not an *ism*. The major misunderstanding is to transform into an *ism* what wasn't at all an *ism*. I hate *isms* because I'm not a theorist.

The second thing I have to say is that unavoidably and inevitably the way a work is introduced into an alien country is necessarily linked with certain mistakes, and I assume this. I have no protestation against this. Finally, if I'm not comfortable, I have to stay in my country, and that's all. So there's a problem in the immigration of a way of thinking, and necessarily the reception is strange. For example, here in the United States I was received as the theoretician of postmodernity and as the postmodernist—oh, my god! For me *The Postmodern Condition* is the worst book I ever wrote, but it was the only one having a certain reception. I don't know why; I can't explain why. My wish is that those people who have the generosity to give some attention to my work would please read other things than this horrible book, because it was just a passage for me. But even so, I was obliged to come back to this question in a second book, *The Postmodern Explained to Children*, and I just published a third book called *Postmodern Moralities*. I'm obliged to do this in order to maintain or to find certain directions in the use of this word. So, I'm ready to be open to a discussion about this question, and I don't want to negate it. But, nevertheless, it's not my real question. I think that the questions you asked, particularly at the beginning of this interview, were closer to my concerns.

❦ ❦ ❦

J. Hillis Miller

Q. Do you consider yourself a writer?

A. I never thought of myself as a writer, though, like a lot of teachers of literature, I had the idea when I was a teenager that I was going to write poetry or novels or something but soon found I had no aptitude for that at all. My writing is an adjunct to teaching. Though it's something I do seriously, I think *writer* is too big a word for what I do.

Q. Would you describe your writing process?

A. The computer transformed my life. There was a period a long time ago when I wrote on a typewriter and then revised with pen, writing things up and down the margins and on the backs of the pages. Then there was a long period, essentially while I was at Yale, when I wrote longhand in notebooks. That allowed me to revise on the page and on the back of the page. (If you were to see those notebooks, you'd find them totally illegible.) Then I would read the manuscript onto a tape; it would be typed by a secretary; then I would revise it; and it would have to be typed again. With a computer, I shortcut all those procedures. I write a draft on the computer (I use a Macintosh) and revise it myself on the computer very extensively, both as I go along and later on when I come back to it. These revisions are "extensive" in that they're changes in individual sentences: cutting long sentences into two or three short sentences, rearranging phrases, moving them around, and so on. The computer has made my revision process longer and more complicated than it was because I'm not inhibited by the necessity of having it typed over again. Of course, all those stages of revision are completely lost; there's no trace of the earlier stages.

Q. Do you believe that academic writers should not cross disciplinary borders?

A. I have a strong commitment to the notion that good writing differs not only for different purposes but in different professional areas. The justification for having writing across the curriculum is that assumptions about what constitutes, say, a good and effective engineering report differ from those about a good essay in art history or anthropology. Good writing goes beyond getting the grammar right. Somebody in an English department really doesn't know what the rules are about writing in the different fields; it's hard to learn these because there are built-in conventions and so on. Nevertheless, one could say *that* ought not to prohibit somebody trained in one discipline from, however modestly and tentatively, dealing with texts in another discipline, and often that person will see some things that wouldn't be seen within the conventions of the primary discipline. So the answer to your question about border crossing is yes and no.

Q. Are there any misunderstandings of your work that you'd like to address now?

A. Sometimes in reviews people have cited things I have said that were intended as ironic or as the miming of somebody else's position as though they were my opinions. Sometimes this is done disingenuously. You take a passage out of context. Miller says this and you quote it. However, if you look back at the context, Miller wasn't really saying this at all; he was saying something like, "People say" or "This is a position"—and that ought to be clear. On the one hand, you point out that this sentence does appear in that essay or in that book; on the other hand, I thought I was making it clear that I was simply saying what my author said: it was Thomas Hardy who was saying this or George Eliot or somebody else, not me. So, I have two exhortations for my readers. First, try to notice whether I might conceivably not be speaking for myself but doing what any literary critic has to do: trying to speak for the author that I'm discussing or even for some imagined position which I'm then going to differ from.

The other exhortation would be to stress again the fact that for me, and I think for my colleagues like Derrida, those theoretical formulations that *can* be detached and are not ironical, that are straight, nevertheless have their meaning only in the context of a reading. The relationship between theory and reading is the really fundamental one, not the detachable theory that you can make into a system. The theoretical statement should always be put back in the context of the reading which—the relationship is a very complicated and uneasy one—both facilitated the theoretical formulation but at the same time isn't quite congruent with it; they're not quite symmetrical, and it's that asymmetry between reading and theory that seems to me fundamental to the nature and function of literary theory. Theory is never fully sponsored or generated or supported or confirmed by the reading; far from it: the reading always does something to the theoretical formulation and at the same time generates new theoretical formulations which have to be modified then in their turn. So a theory is never something that's fixed once and for all, and the thing that alters it is more reading. I think that's often forgotten, perhaps inevitably, in the attempt to reduce my work or somebody else's work to a handy set of theoretical formulations. That's certainly true with Derrida. People will say that Derrida talks about "the free play of language in the void" or something, and you go back and find he's really talking about Lévi-Strauss in that passage and the formulation is only made possible by the reading of the particular author. I think it's often forgotten in what you might call pedagogical accounts of Derrida, accounts used in teaching him, that almost all his work is the reading of some text or other. That's certainly true of my own work.

❧ ❧ ❧

Chantal Mouffe

Q. Do you think of yourself as a writer?

A. Well, I certainly would like to think of myself as a writer, and in a certain sense I do. In fact, before studying philosophy and losing some of my writing skill, I very much wanted to be a writer. That's what I dreamed of when I was an adolescent. There are two obstacles preventing me from becoming the kind of writer that I would like. The first is precisely the fact that I do philosophy. I know that some people (I'm thinking of Derrida) can do both. Engaging in some kind of argument through my philosophy very much describes my style of writing. I used to write much better before. But probably the most serious obstacle is the question of language. I can think of myself as a writer when I write in French, but not when I write in English. I can write in English and in Spanish (I'm basically trilingual), but when I write in English, I write in a very different way: I'm much more matter of fact, I stick to the argument, and there are lots of things concerning style that I can't really do in English. Unfortunately, from the point of view of writing, I write more and more in English. I used to write in French and then have my articles translated into English, but of course that's not very convenient. Now, if I'm writing for an English journal, I write in English; if I'm writing for a French journal, I write in French. And I realize there's a big difference. When I write in French, I can write in a much nicer way, and there are lots of things that I can say in French that I can't say in English. So, when I'm writing in English, I don't think, unfortunately, that I'm much of a writer.

Q. You have coauthored numerous works with Ernesto Laclau. Do you see collaborative work as a *political* choice?

A. In the abstract, I'm in favor of collaborative work; but to be absolutely honest, when Ernesto and I decided to write a book together, it was not at all for any political reason that we thought it was good to do collaborative work. In a sense, I wouldn't even say it was a choice. We felt that we *had* to do it. It was important to us because we felt that we were both interested in the same kind of problems and that our two approaches needed to complement each other. In a sense, I felt that what I wanted to say I could not really say on my own, and I think Ernesto felt the same. We felt that by putting our two skills and points of view together we could make an argument that neither of us would have been able to make alone. I must say, though, that many of my feminist friends were against our collaboration. They said, "Be careful in writing with a man. You will see that he's going to receive most of the credit, especially given the order of your names." They were really saying that I should not do it, but I felt that it was not a choice, that we were compelled to do it. So I don't want to say that we made a political choice. It wasn't like that.

Q. You say in *The Return of the Political* that "To defend political liberalism and pluralism within a perspective which is not rationalist, we have to see parliament not as the place where one accedes to truth, but as the place where it ought to be possible to reach agreement on a reasonable solution through argument and persuasion, while being aware that such agreement can never be definitive and that it should always be open to challenge. Hence the importance of re-creating, in politics, the connection with the great tradition of rhetoric, as suggested by Chaim Perelman." In what ways is this rhetorical model different from consensus-based models that have been criticized as being exclusionary, silencing minority viewpoints?

A. First, we should realize that there are different possible readings of Perelman. For instance, the Habermasians read him in a way that puts much more emphasis on the possibility of an inclusive consensus than I do. Everything hinges on the way one understands what Perelman means by "universal audience." The Habermasians believe that such an audience potentially exists and that we can speak to it. In my reading, this is not Perelman's view. What he says is that there are some disciplines like philosophy that by their very nature—what Wittgenstein would call their "grammar"—need to address themselves to the universal audience *as if there were such a thing*. But I think that Perelman makes it clear that there are always different conflicting conceptions of this universal audience and that therefore there cannot be such a thing. If one accepts this interpretation, Perelman's conception of consensus has to be envisaged in a different way, one that does not conflict with the view I'm advocating.

It's not that I'm opposed to the idea of consensus, but what needs to be put into question is the nature of consensus because I think that every consensus is by nature exclusionary. There can never be a completely inclusive consensus. I would say that the very condition of the possibility for consensus is at the same time the condition of the impossibility of consensus without exclusion. We can find this same idea in Derrida, but Foucault is the one who made it very clear. It's important to realize that in order to have consensus there must be something that is excluded. So the question is not to say that therefore we're not going to seek consensus. That's where I would differ with Lyotard. I think we need in politics to establish consensus on the condition that we recognize that consensus can never be "rational." What I'm against is the idea of "rational" consensus because when you posit that idea, it means that you imagine a situation in which those exclusions, so to speak, disappear, in which we are unable to realize that this consensus that you claim to be rational is linked with exclusion. And rhetoric is important here. But it must be understood that this is the way in which we are going to try to reach some kind of reasonable agreement—"reasonable" meaning that in certain circumstances this is how a political community, on the basis of a certain principle or something it values, is going to *decide* what is acceptable; but this process can never coincide with "rational" consensus. It is always based on a form of exclusion.

So, to come back to Perelman, when we are going to try to establish this form of consensus—in fact, to define what the common good is, because that's what is at stake in politics—we can't do without this dimension on the condition that we recognize that there is no such thing as a *universel auditoire* or the common good and that it's always a question of hegemony. What is going to be defined at the moment as the common good is always a certain definition that excludes other definitions. Nevertheless, this movement to want a definition of the common good, to want a definition of a kind of consensus that I want to call "reasonable" in order to differentiate it from "the rational," is necessary to democratic politics.

Q. For those who want to move decisively in the direction of radical democracy, what do you see as the role of the critical intellectual in promoting the radical project of democracy?

A. It depends on what we understand by "move decisively." If we mean decisively in the sense that it's something that cannot be overturned, I don't think there is ever the possibility of moving in that way; but if by that we mean strong progress in that direction, this is different. I see intellectuals as the ones who elaborate and provide the vocabularies that then can be appropriated by people in order to give some thought to their experience so that they can transform their relations of subordination and oppression. For instance, in radical democracy it's important to formulate conceptions of equality and liberty in order to allow for a new common sense about equality and liberty to be defined. At this precise moment, the task of the intellectual is particularly crucial. We are facing a big deficit of these kinds of new vocabularies, and we are at a moment in which the hegemony of neoliberal discourse is so strong that it seems as if there is no alternative. Unfortunately— and I am speaking of Western Europe—many socialist parties seem to have been convinced of that. What's happening with Tony Blair in Britain is very much the acceptance of the dominant discourse of neoliberalism and of Thatcherism and the redefinition of the objective of the left *within* those parameters. There seems to be no alternative vocabulary. There seems to be no other way to think about this issue, and this is linked to the crisis of social democracy, the crisis of the communist model. Those are vocabularies that do not have any purchase on people's struggles, so the only kind of political language present today is neoliberalism.

There's a real lack of imagination on the point of view of left-thinking intellectuals in creating new vocabularies that will make possible a radical democratic hegemony. If we think, for instance, of what has been happening with neoliberalism, this neoliberal hegemony has been a long time in the making. In fact, there have been people like Friedrich Hayek and Milton Friedman since the 1940s; when there was a stronger social democratic hegemony, they were completely marginalized. They were in fact as marginalized in a sense as we radical democrats are today. Nevertheless, they organized themselves, they created the Mont Pelerin Society, and they slowly began to develop ideas that at some point in the '70s came to be appropriated by movements like Thatcherism and like Reaganism in America in order to give a new form to the political experience and to create new forms of subjectivities. What is missing today is an effort by radical democratic forces to begin to elaborate alternative vocabularies in order to undermine the hegemony of neoliberalism. When I say "vocabularies," of course, I'm not speaking only in terms of linguistics; it also means thinking about what kind of institutions and what kind of practices could be the ones in which new forms of citizenship could exist and what form of grassroots democracy could be conducive to the establishment of this kind of radical democratic hegemony. That's basically what intellectuals should be doing in my view.

Q. Are there any specific misunderstandings of your work that you'd like to address at this time?

A. There have been so many; let me just mention three. One is the question of the economy. That's clearly a widespread misunderstanding—that we are abandoning the question of class, abandoning the question of economy. All our development of hegemony has been to say that we need to articulate the struggle around issues of class with struggles against sexism and racism. So the economy is very much present in our work. That's basically why we define ourselves as post-Marxists. We think that there is something from the teaching of Marx that we want to keep because it's very important and we can't abandon. The second point—which again I find difficult to see how people cannot understand, particularly after the explanation we gave in "Post-Marxism Without Apologies"—is the question of our discourse being idealistic. We've tried often and repeatedly to insist that by "discourse" we don't just mean something related to speech and writing but something similar to what Wittgenstein meant by language games. It's something composed of practices, institutions, discourse; it is something that is very very material. But apparently people can't take the point, and they go on saying that this is an idealistic view. They want to say it's not materialist and that we don't take into account something like reality. Again, this is a basic misunderstanding that is the origin of many criticisms.

The third one, which I also find difficult to understand because I've so often been arguing precisely the contrary, concerns the question of pluralism. We've been accused of defending some kind of total pluralism. We are presented as defending some kind of extreme postmodernism for which there's no way of thinking about any kind of structure. In many papers and conferences I've said that I want to distinguish our form of pluralism both from the liberal view of interest group pluralism and also from what I call some extreme forms of postmodernism. I've been arguing that we need to be able to distinguish between differences that do exist but should not exist. We should fight against them because those differences are based on relations of subordination; and there are differences that do not exist but should exist because it's precisely by the nonrecognition of those differences that relations of subordination are created. But of course it means that not all differences are to be valued and it's not a total pluralism. I've made this argument in very many places. Nevertheless, I quite often see critiques that say I'm defending some kind of extreme pluralism. Those are probably the three more common misunderstandings. I can think of many others, but these probably are the more important ones to consider because they are saying exactly the contrary to what I think.

Avital Ronell

Q. Do you consider yourself a "writer"?

A. In a certain way that question might be too masculinist for me because it suggests some kind of volition, agency, control at the wheel of fortuna or destiny. I would say that I have figured myself as a kind of secretary of the phantom. I take dictation. I would say also that one doesn't call oneself a writer: one is called, or one is convoked to writing in a way that remains mysterious and enigmatic for me. There was nothing that was going to determine this kind of activity or passivity—we still have to determine what writing is, of course. But sometimes I can, in a way, identify with the figures of "writing being" (*Schriftstellersein*) that Kafka threw up. For example, that of Gregor Samsa, who is this little unfigurable, monstrous fright for his family and workplace, and who has to stay in his room, kind of locked up, flying on the ceiling and attached to the desk. *There* is a figure with which I have repeatedly identified—which is to say, there's something monstrous and a little shameful involved in writing, at least in terms of social pragmatics. This sort of logic of the parasite is probably eventually why I wrote about the drug addict and the writer as figures, often paradoxically, of social unreliability, even where their greatest detachment produces minor insurrections, political stalls, and stammers in any apparatus of social justice.

Q. In the introductory remarks to the interview you did with Andrea Juno in *Research: Angry Women,* you are referred to as an "ivory-tower terrorist." Are you comfortable with that label? Does it seem accurate?

A. These are questions about naming and location, and in this regard neither term is acceptable. The ivory tower is something that I have never been embraced by, or possibly even seen; it is a phantasm. And "terrorist" would imply a kind of being that is single-minded and fanatically set on a goal. By contrast, I would be too dispersed, self-retracting, and self-annulling in the way I work to be considered a terrorist as such. If anything, I would say that I am a counterterrorist. It is true that I have called for something like an extremist writing. And also I have made hyperbolic attempts to secure the space of academe as a sheltering place of unconditional hospitality for dissidence and insurrection, refutation and un-domesticatable explosions of thought. To the extent that the academy is a mausoleum, it tends to expect the reverence due the dead, and my irreverent type of reverence seems to set off, in those describing what I do, some explosive language. But I would also say, in a more general and gendered sense, that very often women who have a somewhat original bent are institutionally psychoticized and isolated. They tend to be structurally positioned as dangerous creatures, so there is always a SWAT team of academic proprietors closing in on them. In this sense, I can see how the "terrorist" appellation might have grown on me or been pinned on me. But it comes from the institutional space and not from me. I was tagged.

There's also this: While I was at Berkeley, I was close friends with Kathy Acker and Andrea Juno. *Mondo 2000* declared us the "deviant boss girls of a new scene," models of subversion, and so on. That little community may have provoked some politicized assertions, marking the way the three of us would stage ourselves publicly and kick ass in a certain way. In this regard, I think one would want to look more closely at the possibility or impossibility of friendship in academia, and what it implies. Who are your friends? How does friendship set up (or subvert) a transmission system for the kind of work you do and read? One is often judged by one's public friendships. I was friends with Kathy and Andrea. And I think there was something scary about this little girl gang of troublemaker writers. Certainly, publishing with *Angry Women* did do momentary damage; it dented my career a bit—though it is laughable to offer up an imago of my career as a smooth surface to be dented. It was never not dented: one originary dent. I think colleagues were a little shocked to see me involved with performance artists, recontextualized and reformatted in the space of very angry, very outrageous, shit-covered, dildo-wielding, multi-sexual women. I think there was a gender-genre crossing that probably seemed a little excessive.

Q. Do you consider yourself, in any sense, a rhetorician?

A. First of all, I recognize that this is not a stable appellation; to the extent that rhetoric is a feature of language, one is kind of overwritten by it. I don't see how one could not be inscribed in the rhetorical scene. But, of course, on a more technical and thematic level, I am very attentive to rhetorical maneuvers on different registers of articulation. I tend to try and track something like a rhetorical unconscious in a text. I am very drawn in by that which withdraws from immediate promises of transparency or meaning. For example, I am interested in "anasemia," which is a linguistic force, elaborated by post-Freudian psychoanalysis, that works against normative semantics. I am interested in tracking repressed signifiers, including the relationships between syntactical break-downs and political decisions. I wrote an essay, for instance, about George Bush's inability to produce rhetorically stable utterances, an essay in which I tried to read his rhetorical machine as inexorably linked to the specific kinds of decisions he made and to the reactionary and reactive effects of his administration. Of course, every utterance is susceptible to destabilization, making the itinerary of the question considerably more complicated.

I have been heavily influenced by Paul de Man's work in this area, which leads me to say that one can never be detached from the rhetorical question or from the necessity of a whole politics and history of rhetorical thought, which has been largely re-pressed, or expulsed, or embraced, depending on where you are looking and to whom you are listening. So, indeed, if one is trying to be a rigorous and attentive reader, one has to consider oneself a rhetorician in those senses.

Q. When it first appeared in 1989, the layout and design of *The Telephone Book* were unprecedented in academe. The design of Jacques Derrida's *Glas* is also unconventional; but whereas the simultaneous, multivoiced columns of *Glas* challenge print's linear imperative, *The Telephone Book* seems to break more rules and to be more playfully performative on the whole. What prompted this performative text? What did you hope its performance would accomplish?

A. It's important to note that *Glas* appeared much earlier and has another history of rupture and invention that still calls for analysis. We are all indebted to Derrida's exegetical energy for boosting the desire for the book and for making us interrogate the placid materiality of acts of reading. On another level of your questioning, I would like to recall that all texts are performative. But what I was trying to get at with *The Telephone Book* was the possibility of destroying the book in the Heideggerian sense of accomplishing a certain destruction of its metaphysical folds, enclosures, and assumptions. On the sheerly material level, it provided the first computer virtuoso performance in design. Every page was different, an interpretation of the text. And often I did argue with Richard Eckersley, the marvelous designer, because I felt that he was pulling away from the telephonic logic that I wanted his work to reflect and that he was becoming too autonomous—becoming a computer virtuoso. I didn't want the computer to overtake the telephonic markings that I felt needed to be continually asserted and reasserted. In a sense, we had a war of technologies—of course, over the telephone (I have never met Richard). What I wanted to effect by producing this telephonic logic that would supplant or subvert the book was to displace authorial sovereignty, to mark my place as taking calls or enacting the Heideggerian structure of the call. In other words, I wanted to recede into the place of a switchboard operator, and in that sense emphatically to mark the feminine problematic of receptivity and the place of reception. I was at the reception desk of that which we still call a book, taking the call of the other.

What I wanted to do as well by breaking up the serene, sovereign space of an unperturbed book was to invite static and disruption and noise. I wanted to show—to the extent that one can show this—that the text emerges in a kind of violence of originary interference, a kind of primal buzz. I wanted to inscribe the kinds of wreckage to signification that aren't usually accounted for. And this could be seen as belonging to a kind of post-feminist ethics, too. There is a great logic of disturbance that rattles the text. It doesn't offer the illusion of being from that professorial space of quiet and support and cocooned sheltering. The great male professor seems to me to be served by anything from the wife function to the institutional function. But I wanted this text to be somehow reflective of women's position, of the attempt to write in an institutional war zone, and this included being rattled and taking calls that are not predictable in their arrival, that jam the master codes and jam the switchboard, ever expelling you from the safe precincts of the imagined contemplative life.

When I was at Berkeley and writing this book, whenever someone would ask me what I was working on, I endured a lot of mockery, so I stopped trying to present it. This book was the first theoretical or deconstructive work on technology, and the telephone seemed like an aberrant, abjected object. Why would anyone write on anything so common, absurd, banal, unliterary, or anti-philosophical? Even my colleagues who were historians thought it a preposterous project. Obviously, literary critics didn't see any point to it at all, and the philosophers I hung out with didn't necessarily get it either. There was something that had to remain stealthy and unannounceable about writing on the telephone.

What prompted the project was the surprise that I experienced when I read the interview in which Heidegger was asked to describe the nature of his relationship with National Socialism, and he said he didn't really have a relationship, all he did was take a call from the SA storm trooper. This response appeared to me to be an improbable statement—one, in fact, that might offer an access code, since Heidegger is the thinker par excellence of the call, of the difficult and necessary status of calling. And he is also the one to have pointed to the dangers of technology. He is the one—no matter what one thinks of him, and no matter how one thinks one can evaluate him, his lapses and the ways he has been disappointing (but which philosopher finally hasn't been?). Heidegger certainly is a redneck in many ways and highly problematic as mortals go, but what interested me was this response, which is a very compelling response and non-response at once. If I had been the thinker of the call and had made the call on technology, warning that we live under its dominion in yet undecipherable ways, then I would be clearly codifying my response. I thought he was providing an access code to a truer reading. I went after it.

And that is what prompted me to look to the telephone and to think about its place (or nonplace) or repressed functions in thinking. My question was how you would write the history of a non-relation, which is what Heidegger was asserting. There was a crucial non-relation. It has a history. It's called the telephone. It appeared to require a kind of inclination toward a subterranean history. I asked: What is this place of non-disclosure that doesn't allow for delusions of transparency or immediacy? This non-disclosure in part is why I felt that the book needed to bear the burden of that which resists signification, resists the serene certitudes of reportage or information gathering or knowledge naming that a good many academic books rely upon. I wanted it to come out with a university press because I felt that frame would rattle some cages. There are presumably many advantages to going with a trade or commercial press, but I thought that it had to reside within the university structure, that it actually would do more damage or stir up more trouble if it were to be contained by a university press. By the way, one of my motivating slogans is that a woman should be a *pain in the ass*.

Q. Your work seems consciously to muck with genre boundaries, to operate in the face of inherited borders of thought. Do you set out to break up genres, to force them to collide? Or is it more that you ignore genre boundaries because they don't work for you?

A. I'm keenly aware of the histories and presumptions of that with which I am breaking. Above all, I am a scholar working the German side of things. As for the stability of genres, their boundaries are not as secure as one would think. I am working within a lineage that these genres already prescribe. There is a great insecurity about their limits, and I do try to work at those limits. The history of genre is highly domesticated and meant to suppress anxiety about possible contamination and violation. I am negotiating with what genres know about themselves, which is to say that they can easily collapse, that the border patrol might be dozing off, taking a cigarette break, and then something else occurs that could not have been predicted. I will use a given genre's pretexts and inroads and histories voraciously, but then I'll also invite, in a mood of great hospitality, certain marginalized genres to participate in the "literary critical" move on a text. I work with crime story and drama, and also poetry at some point. In this sense, I am Deleuzean since Gilles Deleuze has called for writing philosophical works in the form of a crime story, zooming in on a local presence and resolving a case. In this connection, I've been very interested in the difference Freud asserts between police work and detective work. (He says sometimes you have to arrest a symptom arbitrarily just to get the analysand to advance in a certain way.) As we know from thematic reflections on the latter, very often the detective has to turn in the badge and assume a different rapport with the truth. This involves solitary tracking. Often one is outcast. Certainly, the figure of the detective is something that fascinates me. Nowadays, of course, we have lesbian detectives on the prowl, looking for some kind of disclosure or going after traces and clues—which is, after all, the position one necessarily finds oneself in when one is engaged in reading.

Q. In the preface to *Finitude's Score*, you suggest that "electronic culture" signals for you a kind of "prosthetic *écriture*" that puts "writing under erasure"; and a few lines later, you make the rather startling statement that you're "writing for writing because it died." Would you elaborate on that a bit? Are you suggesting two different senses of "writing"?

A. That is a very astute observation on your part. Obviously, since Plato all writing has been linked to *techné*, so what I am getting at is a regional difference. Writing was always prosthetic and consistently viewed as a dangerous supplement, as Derrida says. But you're right because there are boundaries and differences to be accounted for. And the kind of writing, I would say, that is associated with imminence and transcendence can no longer be affirmed innocently, as if writing could be capable of true manifestation or disclosure, linked at this point to a kind of transcendental being. Writing is no longer in that kind of association with a privileged locus. The demotion of writing's claims has been thematized by so many writers and observed by so many critics that this project is not, in itself, new. What interests me, though, is the way in which writing has been, in a sense, obsolesced and divested. Of course, one has to be Nietzschean and produce at least two evaluations of that observation because there is something that, despite it all, liberates writing to another realm once its more church- and state-like responsibilities have been suspended. Something else is happening and something else is going on. There is a kind of freedom that writing still says, or tries to say, or can refuse to say. This writing is political, but according to another logic of politics that escapes simple codifications. Nonetheless, writing, in the sense that I have been outlining, with its privilege of transcendence and disclosure, I think can be safely said to have perished, died.

At the same time, what does this mean? Writing never *stops* dying. There is an *endless* ending of writing. Psychoanalysis has been declared dead, too, and so has deconstruction, but, as we know, the dead can be very powerful. Freud illustrates or throws this power switch in *Totem and Taboo*: when the little resentful hordes of brothers get together and kill this powerful father, what they discover is that they are left with remorse and unmanageable haunting and sadness, such that the dead father turns out to be more powerful dead than he ever was alive. He is more alive when he is dead. Thus, to declare writing dead can also, in fact, make it more haunting, more difficult and commanding. It can imply a more pressurized zone of being and a much more intense rapport with that which has died. In making this statement, I'm also aligning myself in some ways with Hölderlin's Diotima: when the philosopher Empedocles commits suicide, Diotima is left behind to read his sandals, which are all that's left of him; they are his remainder. Diotima becomes the reader of this lost foundation or footing that philosophy might have had. Diotima is one exemplary instance of the feminine figure who is left behind as the mourner par excellence and who needs to read the traces and somehow honor them commemoratively. We have this figure also, of course, in the crucifixion of one of our gods. To observe that something has died implies a complicated itinerary of finitude, and it can be an infinite finitude that becomes more and more powerful in its withdrawal, precisely *because* it withdraws.

Q. In *Crack Wars*, you discuss what you call "genuine writing," which you hook up with "'feminine' writing in the sense that it is neither phallically aimed nor referentially anchored, but scattered like cinders." To what extent can this "genuine" writing be conflated with what goes by the name *écriture féminine*?

A. When I use the word "genuine," I am already pointing toward a kind of etymological net that involves "genius" or suggests that there is something that *can't* be proper or genuine. After all, the code of genius is usually reserved for the metaphysical male subject. So I want to bear in mind the irony of "genuine," or the genitality of "genuine," because genuine has to undo itself and dismantle its premises. But what I wanted to underscore when citing this term "genuine" is akin to what I'm underscoring when I use the term "feminine" (and I put them both in quotation marks): that it is not about some recognizably feminine trait. I also use this strategy to rewrite Emma Bovary's name, "*femma*nine," with Emma enacting the femme, and of course with Flaubert being identifiable as Emma, as he himself notes in the famous utterance "*Madame Bovary c'est moi.*" I wanted to show that the predicament of a woman who wants to write but who has nowhere to go and little to do, and who's writing for no one, *counts* for something. I say it is the writer's common lot. The "*femma*nine" is already there in any kind of writing—lurking, latent, showing that all writing is exposed, unsure of its destination, unable to chart its course, unable to know if it is going anywhere but down. Deleuze has said that writing minoritizes the writer and also sets him or her into the condition, or the flow, of becoming-woman. On some level, this phasing out of oneself is what happens to all who write, or to all who are inclined toward writing or who are written up by writing—even written *off* by writing. There is no way for you to think, really, that you know to whom you are writing, or that you are going anywhere, or that you are doing anything, in the classical sense of those terms. Emma's house-wifely psychosis, her loser's sense of having no one to write to, no audience, is to be honored for its particular scenography of abjection, for its critically depressive qualities and properties.

At the same time, doesn't writing turn us all into little house-wives who are sitting home all day? Maybe not with rollers on our heads, but in our little house robes and immobilizations. There is something about being under house arrest, about the solitude, the not knowing what the hell you are talking about.... There are such moments (I hope I am not the only one outing myself here) that occur when you think, in the most expropriated sense, "What am I doing?" At just that moment, when there is nothing holding you up or bolstering your sense of who you are or what you are doing, right *then* you can maybe say that you are a "genuine" writer. So, it is according to that kind of paradoxical itinerary, or in that kind of aporetic rapport with writing, that I was trying to place Emma Bovary, who was kind of my girlfriend for awhile because I really dwelled on and with her. And I got very anxious and upset that all these guys—rather prominent lit crit types—thought they controlled her or understood her and could detach from her general abjection, as though she were simply dismissible and a trash body. Of course, I tried to show to what extent she *is* a trash body. Through her, Flaubert invents the body of the addict. Nevertheless, there was something I wanted to show about her humbling and alienated domesticity that reflects the writer's *common* lot. And no matter how objectionable or easily judgeable she might appear to be, Emma Bovary represents what you become one day when you are a so-called "genuine" writer.

Q. Your approach to writing seems posthumanist, too. Your first book *Dictations: On Haunted Writing* explicitly examines (via the *Conversations* between Eckermann and Goethe) the possibility of writing after the "death" of the author. You redescribe writing from the angle of the possessed and suggest that it "never occurs simply by our own initiative: rather, it sends us. Whether one understands oneself to be lifted by inspiration or dashed by melancholia, quietly moved, controlled by muses or possessed by demons, one has responded to remoter regions of being in that circumstance of nearly transcendental passivity." To a large extent, then, to write is to be a lip-syncher, to take dictation, as you put it earlier. Writing here seems to require a kind of passivity that is not inactive but that is also not, strictly speaking, *active*. In *Crack Wars,* you note that when one writes "there are certain things that force [one's] hand," a "historical compulsion" that "co-pilots [one's] every move." So who is writing when something gets written? Or, more specifically, to what extent are you the author of the books published under the name Avital Ronell?

A. To a very limited extent. As I am speaking, I don't feel contemporaneous with the one who writes because, as we discussed earlier, writing is a depropriative act; it always comes from elsewhere. One is body-snatched, in a trance, haunted. Or, one is on assignment. I use that sense of being on assignment or assigned something to emphasize how I am "called" to writing. I don't know how to locate its necessity. And one doesn't know where the imperative comes from. Nevertheless, one is assigned to it, so that one is always writing at the behest of the Other. At the same time, I am not trying to unload my responsibility here. It is not as though I can say that it comes from elsewhere or that I am merely a zombie of another articulation and therefore that I am in bondage absolutely. There is some of that, of course, but I must still assume the position of a signator because I become responsible to respond to this thing that I am transcribing, assigned to, haunted by. So we're talking about assuming responsibility as a signator, with a signature, but without taking credit. And that, perhaps, is the politics of writing to which I subscribe—which is not to say that I take credit for it. I am always indebted to others. I am always part of a circuitry that speaks through me, writes on me, uses me, and certainly uses my body, which has been "fragilized" and has had to endure quite a bit of suffering in order to allow me to respond to my debt: a matter of my allowance. That is the configuration in which I try at once to name my dispossession, or my possession (I am possessed by the Other), and at the same time to assume responsibility—and yet not suddenly, in absolute, irresponsible contradiction to what I have been trying to say, to take credit for that which traverses me in the work.

Q. How would you characterize the relationship among rhetoric's fundamental elements: the writer, the reader, and the message?

A. Well, understanding the message as the work, I would assume that these fundamental elements are in themselves unstable, sometimes exchangeable or erasable by one another. And I would say that writing alters these elements, doesn't leave them in their place, leaves them expropriated and disfigured, unrecognizable. The work—what you are calling the message—in any case seems to let go of the reader and the writer. In other words, I see the work as solitary, inexhaustible, sovereign—it murmurs incessantly.

But, of course, according to other hermeneutic appropriations, the reader can also produce, or be productive of the work and is inscribed in the work as its codependent, as that on which the work relies in order to be brought into being. This is one type of reading of Hölderlin: the gods—let's call them the message or the *work* or the *writing*—are dependent on mortals, on the poetic word, in order to be brought into time and existence. So these are different configurations in the fundamental triangulation that you set into motion. But in each case, I would say that the writing, the work, produces a type of disfigurement and distortion that requires us to rethink the place, which is never secured, of writer and reader.

Q. Do you consider your writing style political in any sense of that term?

A. To interrogate meaning is a political gesture that forces one to interpret community and sociality in its possibility. In that regard, yes, it has to be viewed as such. Traditionally, communication and community involve gathering around stabilized meanings. So by taking risks—and it is not *I* who is taking risks but rather language is risk-taking and risk-making—by *surrendering* to the risks that linguistic positing inevitably demands of one means, at least at some level, to hear and heed the call to break with the oppressive dragnet of reactionary significations. There is a class struggle in my texts: there's the girl gang speaking, the little gangster, the hoodlum; there's the high philosophical graduate student who studied at the Hermeneutics Institute in Berlin; and there's the more sophisticated Parisian, and so forth. There are different voices, compulsions, denials, and relations that emerge in the texts. But there is the continuity of the more "prolo," proletariat, and very often wise-ass girl who is watching this stuff happening and commenting on it—again, like the chorus or the buffo— who's ironic and whose narcissism involves a kind of sarcastic, biting, meta-critique of what is going on but without ever becoming anti-intellectual. That's important. I never embrace the anti-

intellectual tendencies of the American academy. But, then, my
boundaries for what is intellectual are very, very generous, I think.
A lot belongs to that space.

Indeed, I am always questioning what is proper to meaning and
what is propertied by our estates of meaning, of teaching, and so
on. It is not that I am playing with meaning but that meaning is
playing me, and playing through me, on me, and against me all the
time. I am inscribed in that disjunctive flow of meaning's regi-
men. Again, I want to note that I don't sit there as the pilot in the
great *Star Trek* fantasy, with fabulous equipment, and such.
Actually, even in *Star Trek* they got lost in space a lot. I don't
decide; it decides me, it plays me, and I surrender and listen to it
or take it down, as would a secretary taking shorthand. I suppose
I don't repress it or call in the police to clean up the scene of the
crime.

Q. Your texts are *jarring*; they are in no sense comfortable or
comforting; they jerk the reader around a bit. It is difficult to name
exactly what's going on, but even at the level of the sentence, or
of the phrase, your work delivers a kind of disorienting smack.

A. That is interesting because it's familiar. Very long ago, at the
beginning of my career, when I wasn't getting any jobs and I was
completely destitute and desperate, I told my friend Larry Rickles,
who became the chair of German at the University of California
at Santa Barbara, that I didn't understand why this was happening.
And he said, "You are going to have to become aware of the sheer
radicality of your work, which is in sum an outrage." And that was
the first I had heard of it. There's this little girl in me who just
doesn't get it, who thinks she's really handing in the right
assignment. Of course, we know from Freud and then Lacan that
everything you hand in is your own *caca*. And you're *so proud* of
it. Still, there is this little retarded or naive parasite-being in me
who doesn't know this yet, who doesn't realize it, who thinks she
is so loving, who sees herself opening up to everyone, and who

thinks, "Why are they mean?"

I don't know what this absurd anxiety is about, this desire to be able to say, "Have a nice text." It could be an effect of having been severely undermined. De Man said that I was a "professionally battered woman" before this term came into the public domain. I was beaten to a pulp by all sorts of institutional experiences; for example, I was fired illegally. There is still that part of me, the abused child of academia who wants to be accredited and who wants to be told, "This is highly responsible work; we see you in the tradition of the Romantics and Hannah Arendt; you're in touch with the necessary mutations of your historicity." That part of me appears to persist.

When the *Telephone Book* first came out, I was greatly distressed. I felt exposed, that I wasn't one of "the boys." When I saw the *Telephone Book*, it came to me that I had broken with recognizable norms, and this prompted a narcissistic blowout. I really had a very bad depressive reaction because I felt it wasn't recuperable as typical scholarly work. I guess there is a double compulsion: part of me wants to please and to be institutionally recognized, patted on my back (or ass), but another part of me would feel molested by that kind of recognition. It's actually kind of a class warfare. There is the little bourgeoise who thinks, "Well isn't it time that I got some comfort here?"; and the other street girl who says, "Nah!" So you're right. When you say that this work jerked you around or was jarring, violent maybe, that surprises me, and yet, of course, I was there when it happened.

Q. Are there particular misreadings or misunderstandings that you'd like to address here?

A. You know, I am touched by this question, and I am very sensitive to the kind of rescue mission it entails. At the same time, though, I feel deeply that it is not my place to assume the posture of authority, or to place myself in the control tower that lands the *right* reading, the *right* understanding, and sees to it that certain calamities don't occur. I feel that the work is not mine to correct. When a misunderstanding does come to me in a way that I find intelligible, I try to address it in the next work. Since I question the closure of interpretation, I can't allow myself to slip into the place that would prescribe how texts are meant to be read. I have to rigorously affirm their having been sent and having gone out to do whatever it is they have to do. A text's got to do what a text's got to do. Even if it brings shame upon my name.

The only thing I might signal—and this cannot be corrected, and I can't provide a correctional facility for such critical behavior—is that often, especially coming from England, there will be reviews of my work in which the *guy* will say that I should be beaten for the way I write, or that I should be smacked for this or that. These reviews, that is, involve a supplement of physical abuse. In the early part of my career, I was pushed off podiums and stages; I was interrupted and just largely reviled in the most Ivy Leagued places, the big leagues. Somehow, I provoked violent responses. And this response is just a dimension of my work that probably should not be left out of the picture. These critics and colleagues may want to learn to read their own symptoms, may want to consider why it is that a little girl's work can provoke such reactionary responses. The level of rage that prescribes physical correction and censorship is interesting to note. That's all I'll say. The misunderstandings are probably necessary, and the calls for violence are symptomatic and real. One thread of my narrative entails the continuing saga of a manhandled woman, psychoticized by institutional forms of undermining that do occur. I am fortunate in many ways, though. At times, I feel like a cartoon character. I have survived so many batterings, and I am up again and running—at a slower pace, but after this explosion and that removal of ground, I'm back on the scene. I feel very welcome here in New York, so that's wonderful. But perhaps some readers/critics would like to reflect on the recurring shift to violence, the desire to do violence, to violate this textual body.

❦ ❦ ❦

Richard Rorty

Q. Do you think of yourself as a writer?

A. I enjoy writing, but I have no idea of what the effect of the style
on the audience is. I think, like most people in this line of work,
I write to please myself. I'm conscious of striving after turns
of phrase and that kind of thing. I spend a lot of time polishing
things up.

Q. What is the role of rhetoric?

A. Well, insofar as one defines rhetoric by contrast with logic, I
suppose that the ideal of the logician is to make both metaphor and
idiosyncratic stylistic devices unnecessary. And the kind of attack
on traditional positivistic philosophy of science that we've had in
the last thirty years or so adds up to the claim that not even in
science is there this disjunction between logic and method on the
one hand and rhetoric on the other.

Q. Kenneth Bruffee argues that writing is a "technologically displaced form of conversation." He argues, "If thought is internalized public and social talk, then writing of all kinds is internalized
social talk made public and social again." Does this concept of
writing correspond with your own?

A. What Bruffee says seems true enough, but I'm not sure what it
shows. It comes down to saying that all thought, discourse, and,
a priori, all writing take place in some social context, and that's
certainly true; but I'm not sure what Bruffee would say follows
from this. It doesn't seem to me that one can draw many conclusions about how to write from something that general. There are
all kinds of utterly unconversational modes of exposition that are
handy for some particular pedagogic or other purpose.

Q. Some scholars have used your notions of discourse communities to argue that the job of freshman English is to teach students the discourses of the academic disciplines rather than the traditional "essay" which students are traditionally taught in first-year English. They say, in effect, let's forget the traditional, artificial essay and teach them the normal discourse of whatever field the student is going into.

A. The suggestion that they learn the normal discourse in the field suggests that, as freshmen, they try to pick up the jargon of a particular discipline. It strikes me as a terrible idea. I think the idea of freshman English, mostly, is just to get them to write complete sentences, get the commas in the right place, and stuff like that— the stuff that we would like to think the high schools do and, in fact, they don't. But as long as there's a need for freshman English, it's going to be primarily just a matter of the least common denominator of all the jargon. Besides, I don't see how freshman English teachers are supposed to know enough about the special disciplinary jargon. I think that America has made itself a bit ridiculous in the international academic world by developing distinctive disciplinary jargon. It's the last thing we want to inculcate in freshmen.

   I think of abnormal discourse as a gift of God rather than anything anybody gets educated for or into. It seems to me that the normal division between secondary and tertiary education is and should be the line between getting in on the normal discourse of the tradition in the nation and the community to which you belong, and higher education is a matter of being told about all the alternatives to that tradition, to that discourse. But that isn't necessarily going to move you into one of these alternatives; it's just going to make it possible, if you have an imagination, for that imagination to work.

❦ ❦ ❦

Gayatri Chakravorty Spivak

Q. How do you conceptualize rhetoric?

A. I see rhetoric as I see most other important master words in the tradition of poststructuralist nominalism. Foucault says in *The History of Sexuality* that in order to think power one must become a nominalist; power is a name that one *lends* to a complex network of relationships. In Paul de Man's *Resistance to Theory*, rhetoric is the name for the residue of indeterminacy which escapes the system. In this reading, the idea that rhetoric is tropology is not adequate to the notion that it is the name of what escapes even an exhaustive system of tropological analysis. In Derrida it would be very hard to find a definition of rhetoric that calls it a tropological activity. I think that in Derrida there is no concerted, or organized, use of the word *rhetoric* as there is in de Man. Derrida does not consistently use any master word that enables one to put together a body of definitions as something to be applied. I think the word *rhetoric* serves in the same way or does not serve in the same way in Derrida's writing. I think Derrida uses the word *rhetoric* when he's actually dealing with Greek material, but not otherwise.

Q. Do you think students should be taught to write for general audiences or should they be taught to address audiences familiar with specialized jargon, grammars, and methodologies?

A. I guess I'm a little old-fashioned about this. First of all, in any kind of a course, since writing is a tool that goes across the board, I should care if it's done competently. On the other hand, it does seem to me that it's not a very good idea to teach writing through physics, chemistry courses, and so on, because the teaching of reading cannot be done, let's say, in the "Senate house." Although we do, in fact, read the world as we are engaging in politics, you cannot, in fact, bring the training in reading into the arena where reading is something that is also done. I think there have to be places where you do nothing but the skill, and then the application of the skill develops. I'm not saying that when you teach the skill you should confine yourself to nothing but the skill itself, as a subject matter, but I am saying that when you are actually teaching, when you are actually involved in a major where the teaching of the content is important, you also must emphasize content. I don't know if this is an old-fashioned point of view, but it is certainly my conviction.

❦ ❦ ❦

Jane Tompkins

Q. Do you think of yourself as a writer?

A. Yes I do, but only very recently have I thought of myself that way. It's a great pleasure to think that I *can* think of myself as a writer because, like most people who go into literature, I suppose I admired writers excessively and looked up to them. Although I didn't realize while I was in graduate school and for the first twenty years of teaching that I really aspired to be a writer more than a critic, now that I've made this crossover, I'm absolutely delighted. Let me say, though, that I think it's a false dichotomy: a scholar/critic versus a writer. It's a dichotomy we've been sold in some way by the tradition we work in, and it's not useful to us anymore. One sign that it's no longer useful is the quantity of autobiographical writing that is appearing—not just from women, but from men as well. And men respond to this kind of writing just as much as women do. (Well, maybe not as many men do, but many men respond very positively to it, and some are practicing it.) So, now that I think of myself as a writer, I want to encourage everybody who goes to graduate school and engages in the kind of writing that we do in graduate school to think of themselves that way, too, because I think it can only enhance the reach and quality of the work that gets done.

Q. Would you describe your writing process?

A. Well, once I used to write longhand, and then I used a typewriter, and then (actually fairly early on) I switched to the computer. I was a very slow writer, extremely slow, and I felt that the technology of the computer would allow me to revise better. I was a compulsive reviser, though much less so now than say twelve years ago. I got a computer in 1981, and I got it precisely because I revised so much and therefore had to be constantly retyping. I was looking for something that would relieve me of that. What I found was what everyone told me I would find: that the benefit is not simply in the ease with which you can revise, but rather in what it does to your process of composition. That is, the initial writing itself is freed up by the things the computer makes easy. Whether it's just because of the difference in the writing technology or because (probably more likely) I've had a considerable degree of success (my writing has met with a lot of positive response), I write much more easily now, and sometimes I don't have to revise much at all. So, the *kind* of writer I am has changed with the change in my status and in my self-confidence. My book *West of Everything* was put forward by Oxford for a Pulitzer Prize in the category of nonfiction. I found this out a few weeks ago, and damned if I haven't been able to stop myself from writing since then. I think it's one of maybe hundreds of nominations, but anyway Oxford picked it for *its* submission. I guess what I'm saying is that your writing process, in my experience, is very much a function of your psychological, technological, and other circumstances.

I'm just beginning to change my notion of the role writing has in my life now, and I can't predict exactly how it's going to turn out in the end, but in a sense it's parallel to the change that's taken place in my teaching. Just as I've tried to step back from what I call the "performance model" of *teaching*, where your ego is very much at stake, to a different mode where presumably your ego is not so much on the line (although, in fact, it still is), I've become more aware of the extent to which *writing* for people in our profession is a kind of ego activity. I'm not in the least degree free from that myself, but the recognition that that's the case makes me question somewhat the role that writing has played for me. It may be that I will write less in the future and try to change the arena of my activities from writing to what you might call *action*—that is, doing things. I've been smitten with Natalie Goldberg's books, *Writing Down the Bones* and *Wild Mind*, and insofar as I understand it, writing for her is what she calls "a practice" akin to the practice of meditation. (She's a Zen Buddhist and her whole understanding of what writing is comes out of her Zen background.) In that way of thinking, writing becomes a mode of self-refinement and self-development which is an end in itself, and so the product or performance dimensions of it become secondary or perhaps not important at all. I think all of us in our profession use writing in that way whether we know it or not.

I don't know whether Goldberg talks about this since I haven't read everything in those books, but I've recently come to understand writing as a way that people like us have of taking care of ourselves. When we can't get to our writing, we feel deprived and we feel hungry for it, not just because we're afraid we won't get our articles written so that we won't get our job or our promotion (although certainly those fears apply), but because there's a need that we have to perform this activity *for ourselves*. It's almost like a grooming activity, or something that you do in the mode of self-care, like getting a massage or working out. It's a form of attention that seems to be directed outward toward an object outside of yourself, but somehow the effect strangely is to have attended to yourself in some way. That's the way I'm coming to understand it. To that degree, I don't know that I'll be able to give up writing very easily.

I also see writing as a form of self-development and self-discovery, as a way you can come to know yourself and learn about yourself, or just as a mode of learning pure and simple. In that regard, my sort of proof text is a line from Robert Pirsig's *Zen and the Art of Motorcycle Maintenance*: "The motorcycle you're working on is the motorcycle of yourself." When Pirsig talks in an extended passage in that novel about something he calls "gumptionology," which is the science of what it takes to fix a motorcycle, I read that as being about writing and have always so read it. That approach to writing—that is, you think you're working on the motorcycle and you're really working on yourself—is one that I've recently come to.

I have a writing group that has been in existence for five years now, and those are my "main men," so to speak (they're all women), the people to whom I show my work and from whom I get the feedback that helps me write. This writing group has been an essential aid in pushing me forward in the directions I need to go as a writer, and it has been a continual source of support in the process of composition—a process that otherwise is extremely lonely.

Our format has changed over the years: we expanded from three to four, and that meant some changes; then, because the group was bigger, it wasn't working out so well and we changed again. We meet every two or three weeks at the house of one or another of us. Right now we're in a mode in which we don't read anything in advance; we just bring our work to group. Only two people are on in any given day so that there's enough time to be given to each person's work. Right now we're supposed to keep the meeting to two hours—one person gets an hour and then the other person gets an hour—but it's usually prefaced by a half an hour of conversation in which we try to catch up with one another, find out what's going on in each other's lives, talk department gossip, or say whatever we need to get off our chests. In the very beginning of the group, which I formed as a result of reading Peter Elbow's *Writing with Power*, we had some protocols about the kinds of feedback that were or weren't appropriate to give, and now and then we review this. Basically, people ask for the kind of feedback they want to have on a given day, and they can also ask specific questions that they want us to answer. For all the members, the group has been a mainstay and a wonderful help, but this isn't to say that the group hasn't had a lot of problems and that we don't have to stop from time to time and talk about what's been going on among us and what our gripes are and what we'd really like to be getting out of it. We're about to do that again when we all get back from vacation.

Q. So there's continual attention paid to the social dynamics of the group as well as to the writing that's brought into the session.

A. That's only slightly overstated. That is, we have slowly learned that it is necessary to pay attention to those dynamics, that they won't just take care of themselves, that things build up under the surface and we have to talk them out and deal with them one way or another. I think we're getting to the point where we can anticipate them a little better. I strongly recommend writing groups as a way not just to write but to exist in the academy. It gives you a kind of base of support that is both personal and institutional, as well as continual "real world" feedback for what you're doing. Also, the earlier you can show something to somebody, the better off you are as far as I'm concerned. We show each other the absolute raw stuff as it comes out, and that's the best way to do it.

ờ ờ ờ

STEPHEN TOULMIN

Q. Do you think of yourself as a writer?

A. Yes, I suppose I think of myself as a writer. I get more direct and intense satisfaction out of writing something to my own satisfaction than I do out of, for instance, teaching; and if the choice is between being a writer or being a teacher, I'm a writer. I'm not sure that just being a writer is an honorable way of spending a whole life, but that's another matter.

Q. Would you describe your writing process?

A. Well, I've been writing for more than forty years, and the process has changed (some people never leave the quill pen behind). I wrote out my first ethics book with pen and ink. What I tend to do most often now (though not with the most difficult material) is to talk a draft into a tape recorder, have that transcribed onto a Macintosh disk, and then do the really hard work, which is the editing, on the word processor. To me, this is the most satisfactory, up-to-date technique given what's available. I underline, though, that the really hard work is the editing. When I wrote things with ink or when I had a typist who typed things out, I was inhibited because it embarrassed me very much to send the same thing back for retyping seven or eight times just because I wanted to rephrase things or to move a clause from one place to another. So, I find the word processor a great invention from the moral as well as the technological point of view: I don't have the sense that I'm exploiting the secretarial help in the way I did. Let me say, too, that by and large I never begin to write anything until I have the whole thing worked out. I don't embark on a writing project to see how it looks. I typically, even in my books, even in the *Cosmopolis* book, have a pretty accurate idea about what will go into every stage.

Q. So, you give a great deal of thought to the subject before actually dictating a text.

A. It's not that I think about it; it's much more like architecture. I have to have a sense of the architectonic of it, a sense of where I'm headed and how it's all fitting together. Obviously, some of that goes down on paper or in the computer in the form of headings and a sort of blocking out of rough chapter sections and so on, but the actual writing process, which may be the dictating process, really begins only at the point at which I know what the entire opus is supposed to be. I said a moment ago that editing is the most important factor. Having lived all these years with the texts of philosophers, let me say that there are few things more irritating in reading a philosopher (well, it's partly irritation, partly the joy of discovery) than when you read a text for the seventh time and suddenly realize what it is the writer is trying to say. Especially if it is a very good point that you've previously come to recognize for *yourself*, it's a little irritating that it hadn't been made clear that this is what the person was saying. I have this trouble particularly with a man I immensely admire: John Dewey. I have a sense sometimes that he just kept writing and periodically tore off the lengths and sent it to the printer. I'm quite sure that Dewey didn't do what I do, and I almost mean this dead literally (though a lot of it actually goes on in my head subvocally rather than vocally): I go through all my material repeatedly to see how it will *sound* to a reader and how the rhythms of the prose will come out and contribute to the reader's understanding. The effect of this is that a lot of people say to me, "Oh Stephen, you're so lucky to be able to write so clearly." To which I state Toulmin's Law of Composition: *The effort the writer does not put into writing, the reader has to put into reading.* The only trouble is that since I put immense effort into the editorial stage so as to make sure not only that I have said what I wanted to say but that it comes off as having a kind of natural rhythm, I rather resent being told that this came easily.

Revision is especially important in philosophy, where obscurity is regarded as a mark of profundity. As a result of deliberately avoiding being obscure, philosophers have at any rate made *some* effort to write with non-Germanic clarity, and thank God on the whole this has been part of a longstanding tradition among philosophers of English origin from John Locke and David Hume on.

Q. What makes a text persuasive?

A. I have to start with a prefatory remark. We find ourselves in a situation in which the word *context* is used to mean two quite different things: on the one hand, the larger text of which a particular text is a part, the other bits of text which are around it; on the other hand, the situation, the situation into which a text is put. I have to be rather careful because in writing *Cosmopolis*, at a certain stage about halfway through it, I realized that all the things I'd said about "decontextualization" and "recon-textualization" were really "desituation" and "resituation." I suppose it might have been a good idea if I'd gone through it with my word processor's search and replace; however, my editor convinced me that people wouldn't be grateful with being stuck with neologisms and that if there is this ambiguity in words like *decontextualize*, we're stuck with it for the time being. With that said, I believe every text has to be understood in relation to a situation. In this I agree with Habermas that all knowledge is related to a human interest of one kind or another. This human interest may be that of molecular biologists, in which case what makes a text persuasive has something to do with the role of that text in whatever conceptual clarification and refinement is occurring in a particular corner of molecular biology. And that's not a simple matter; it isn't a matter of finding out that two and two make four. The whole of philosophy of science is concerned with deciding what's at issue when a new paper is regarded as having made a deep and important contribution to molecular biology, for instance. Obviously, the less well-defined the situation within which a text is made public and the shared goals of the author and the audience toward which the publication of the text is intended to make a contribution, the harder it is to say what makes something persuasive. When Mr. Churchill gave speeches in the House of Commons in the early 1940s, they were, as I recall, wonderfully persuasive, but in a different kind of way from the texts in molecular biology. We can reread those speeches now and admire the craftsmanship involved in their composition and the flawless actor's way in which throw-away phrases and such things were inserted, but when we reread them now there's nothing to say they're persuasive because the occasion for persuasion has passed. We can see what *might* have made them persuasive, but that's a piece of historical reconstruction now.

Q. So there's nothing inherent in a speech or a text that ensures persuasion; it's always contingent upon a specific context or situation.

A. All language functions in situations. I'm still enough of a Wittgensteinian to believe that there has to be a *Lebensform* [life-form] in order for there to be a *Sprachspiel* [language game]. Unless there are human beings engaged in shared activities, there is no scope for language to be put to use in a way that will convey anything.

Q. What role do you see rhetoric playing in a postmodern age?

A. I think "rhetoric" is kind of a code word. When I refer to my own work as sketches for another organon, what goes with this is a sense that what needs reviving is not just rhetoric but all the bits of the organon that are not analytic. And I think theoretical philosophy as it has existed since the seventeenth century has generally attempted to confine the discussion of argumentation and the validity of arguments to the zone occupied by the *Prior and Posterior Analytics* of Aristotle. Why? For the very good reason that it appeared that one could keep those under sufficient control to say (roughly speaking) that there was only one valid answer to any given question, and only one valid form. Whether the argument was valid or not is a question that can be established and to which the answer can be given without peradventure, whereas once you get into ethics, politics, poetics, rhetoric, and the other things that Aristotle also regards as worth including in his entire series of linked projects, the thing becomes inescapably hermeneutic. So for me, what we call "rhetoric" has to be understood as including dialectic, topics, all those bits of the discussion about argumentation that are not analytic. Whether it's prudent to go on calling these things "rhetoric" when there are still many people for whom the word *rhetoric* has all kinds of bad overtones, is another question.

Q. Are there any criticisms or misunderstandings of your work that you would like to address at this time?

A. I have shamelessly failed to pay attention to criticism of my work. I have a colleague at the University of Pittsburgh, Adolf Grunbaum, who is so hurt by criticism that if you write even a friendly three-page note in some journal he'll come back with a twenty-one page correction of your misunderstandings of his position. He was once sleepless for a long time because *Philosophy of Science Quarterly* had devoted a whole issue to his ideas, and there in print were all of these papers by people who he thought were his friends and who thought of themselves as his friends, but the papers were so full of misunderstandings that he didn't see how he would ever succeed in correcting them. It's unfair of me to cite Adolf; he's a nice fellow but feels he can't let anything pass. I'm absolutely the opposite: I quite shamelessly let everything pass because I'm much more interested in writing the next book. To return to the very first thing we were talking about, I know well that I put as much work as I possibly could into making what I said plain and intelligible. And I do find that a surprisingly large number of people turn out to have read my work and understood perfectly well what I was saying. On the whole, the people who are captious are those who have their own ax to grind. They use what they take my views to be, not always in as friendly a spirit as Charlie Willard, as a whipping post of some kind or another. It's all a question of priorities. By the time the criticisms of any one book come out, I've moved into another area, and I feel disinclined to go back and root around in a field I've left.

Slavoj Žižek

Q. Do you consider yourself a writer?

A. No. No, in the sense that for me a writer is someone for whom style matters. In an almost old-fashioned, metaphysical sense, I am obsessed with the idea that I have to render, to transmit. I don't have an aesthetic attitude toward writing, in the sense of caring how I place words and so on; the only thing that matters to me is whether my point comes through. There is even, I would say, a certain cruelty or ruthlessness in it, in that I really don't care *how* my prose is formulated. I'm never concerned about whether it would sound better if I'd phrase it in a more elegant way. The only thing that attracts me at the level of style is that from time to time I try to introduce some self-ironical inside joke. For example, all my friends know that I have three or four repetitive turns of phrase that I use all the time. The one I use most often is "on the contrary" or "in contrast"; the other one is "in the first approach it seems to be such and such, but if you look closer you'll see that it's actually something else." That's as far as I go.

I feel a certain ruthlessness about writing: I try to identify myself as a thinking machine. Maybe this is connected with the fact that from my youth I was never tempted to write literature or, God forbid, poetry. There is something in my nature that absolutely prohibits it. I found it obscene, as if for me writing poetry would be masturbating in public, exposing myself too much. This is why, even with authors like Jacques Derrida (whom I am in dialogue with all the time and appreciate very much), I sometimes have this problem: even though I admire a lot of his essays, I nonetheless tend to skip the first third of them—which, as you know, is usually the part before he passes on to the argument. Before finally getting to the point, you have to go through certain ballet pirouettes, like "Am I writing this article or is this article writing me?" That's my attitude: pure, cruel self-instru-mentalization. Maybe my effort to erase traces of myself from my writing is part of my obsessional nature. I don't want to be present in the events that I participate in. I try to become invisible. For example, when I stay at a hotel and I must leave the room for a couple of hours, I try to make it as if I hadn't been there. This has more to do, maybe, with psychoanalytic questions such as whether I perceive myself as someone who shouldn't exist—but that's too existential to bring up at this time.

Q. Tell us about your writing process? Do you revise? Use a computer?

A. Computers were invented for me—by God or whomever. I cannot even imagine how I functioned before them. You should know two things about my style of writing. First, I am absolutely horrified of the writing process, so I have an obsessional strategy: I divide the process in two. Initially, I just put down my notes. I say to myself, "Let's formulate this a little bit, but this is not yet 'writing proper'; I'm simply putting down my notes." Then at some point I say to myself, "Now, everything is already written; it's just a matter of composing it." The writing process is an absolute horror for me; it's an unimaginable anxiety to say to myself that I am really writing. It has to be either preparation or maybe just what in psychoanalytic dream theory is called "secondary elaboration," where you just put the finishing touches on—but never "writing." So that's one feature of my writing process. The other is that I never write in my head. I don't begin with an entire line of thought in my head. I write in complex units—let's call them "abstract units"—in which each unit develops one line of thought, usually in three to four pages, and these units more or less correspond to the subchapter headings in my books. I simply write these units and then it's a matter of how to combine them into larger units. But, again, I never start in advance with a whole line of thought. So, I have an idea and the main task is to make sure that this idea will get through. This is why I don't consider my using a lot of examples to be part of a "style." To me, it's simply to make completely sure that the idea comes through.

And then it's only a matter of combining these ideas. That's how I do it. You can imagine how much I had to copy, cut, and paste—using scissors and tape—before personal computers, so PC's come in very handy. Again, for me the act of writing is an absolute horror. I try to do everything to avoid it.

Q. Do you imagine a particular audience when you write?

A. No. That's very interesting, but no—except in a very general way, in the sense that maybe some people think that I enjoy all those obscene examples I use, but it's the other way around. Perhaps it's a strangely perverse universe, but I really enjoy writing abstract theory, but then I feel a strange pressure to add all those examples as the—how do you call it?—frosting on the wedding cake.

Q. In "Is it Possible to Traverse the Fantasy in Cyberspace?" you discuss the obverse of "interactivity," the phenomenon called "interpassivity." The distinguishing feature of interpassivity is that "in it, the subject is incessantly—frenetically even—*active,* while displacing on to another the fundamental passivity of his or her being." To avoid the clichéd example of interpassivity—the canned laughter on a sound track, where the television in effect laughs for you—you point to the popular Japanese toy, the *tamagochi,* a "virtual pet" that constantly places "demands" on its caretaker. Would you say that interpassivity is a characteristic specifically of the postmodern condition, or of the human condition in general?

A. As with fetish, at a certain level it is constitutive of the human condition as such. I claim that a certain interpassivity is involved in the very Freudian notion of fundamental fantasy (I try to develop this in *The Plague of Fantasies*). My Slovene friends did inquiries into what extent a certain caricatural image is true—namely, now that we are in Slovenian capitalism, all the nouveau businessmen like to go to prostitutes (and there is a tremendous market for them) to be beaten. These hyperactive businessmen need to fantasize about being reduced to total passivity. I am just trying to generalize this phenomenon: in order to be active, you have to fantasize about another scene where you are reduced to the utmost passivity. This is why in a new text of mine (which I worked on like crazy last year and almost collapsed doing it) I talk about the movie *The Matrix*. I was not as charmed as some people were with *The Matrix*, but the one scene that I admired involves how you think you are active, but then you awaken and see that you are in a fetal, baby-like position. It's the only scene that I like in the movie; it's when Keanu Reeves awakens and sees thousands of fetuses. The movie is very close to the truth; the only thing you have to do is to turn the terms around: it's not that we imagine ourselves to be active in virtual manipulated reality but really we are; the true problem is that while we are active we fantasize that we actually occupy a passive position. What you ideally achieve in psychoanalytic treatment is precisely that you no longer need that passive support. But what interests me most are the recent political uses of it. Why does interpassivity play a more crucial role today? Precisely because of the hyper-frenetic rhythm of today's society where this interpassive dream is needed more than ever. It can even have rather comical forms. For example, one of the shocking experiences of my political experience in Slovenia was to discover that it's not we pure intellectuals who believe in our ideals versus corrupted politicians. The more politicians were corrupt, the more they needed us as the Other, as the naive believer. They needed an Other: "We are corrupt but at least you believe." They needed the Other, the one who sincerely believes. Or there's the example that I mention all the time: the typical Western progressive academic who needs the dream that there is another place where they have the "authentic" revolution so that they can be authentic through an Other. But, I don't think we can limit this to something specific only to our Western society.

There are other, even more interesting examples that I haven't used. For example, have you noticed what strange things are going on in today's art? I hate art. Visual art and I just do not agree. It's even worse than cinema. You know how it is with cinema and me. I'm going to say this officially, so you can use it. I don't care. After that article in *Lingua Franca* where I was unmasked, I don't care! Did you know that I have not seen a lot of the films that I write about? For example, in *Enjoy Your Symptom* there is a long chapter on Rossellini. I haven't seen the films. I tried to, but they are so boring. They're so boring! So this is, you see, interpassivity. I said, "I will write about them, but I don't care to see them." But seriously, I think that what is crucial in art today is the new role of curators—a role that is totally different from before. Curators play a double role. On the one hand, artists themselves are aware that today art needs a theoretical background. It's no longer a direct relationship: I paint something nice so that you will enjoy it. The more the artists despise the theorists, the more they need them. I experienced this innumerable times. An artist attacked me—"You produce theory, so you don't know what art is"—and then in the end asked, "but would you nonetheless write something for my catalog?" There is a terrible need of legitimization, and the curators serve this role. The curator is supposed to be someone who understands theory and who then makes an exhibit; it's a much more active role. Today, more and more curators directly order artists to create specific things, or they even directly create objects of art, like in an exhibition, apart from the works of art which are created as such, they will place some objects. For example, think of someone like Joseph Beuys; it's difficult to say where he stopped being an artist and where he started being a curator with all his ready-made stuff. On the other hand (now we enter interpassivity), how does the typical corrupted visitor of New York galleries act? Today, there are so many exhibitions, you don't really have the time to see all the pictures. Nonetheless, people, intellectuals, discuss them. It's as if the curator were the one who really had the time to see all of it (and possibly to enjoy it) for you so that you are allowed to discuss it: "No, that's crap," or "I like that artist."

It's a little bit like dealing with Claude Lanzmann's *Shoah*. I know that *Shoah* is almost untouchable; you are not allowed to criticize it because it's the "ultimate movie." To me, this iconoclastic prohibition is a little bit ironic. It's like, "Thou shalt place no other movie beside me." It's a very strange film. It's so long—nine hours—that it tries to make you feel guilty by its very form. I will not name names, but I can guarantee that a lot of people who wrote eulogies praising the movie haven't seen all of it. Not only do you feel guilty about the Holocaust, but you also feel guilty for not seeing the entire film, which makes you feel even more guilty for the Holocaust. It's kind of a super-ego structure built into the very film itself. So here is another element of interpassivity, where an ideal passive position is constructed and simply presupposed. You don't see a film like *Shoah*; you discuss it. You presuppose another ideal passive viewer, though I doubt if there are many of them.

Unfortunately, this is more and more the phenomenon today. For example, in philosophy there are books that are big hits but that are not read. In Germany, the author of *Critique of Cynical Reason* (which was his first big hit), Peter Sloterdijk, has now published a book that is a big bestseller. It will be in a couple of volumes (he's published only the first two), and each volume is between eight hundred and one thousand pages. People talk about this book, but there is a big discussion in Germany about whether anyone has really *read* the book. (There is a theory that there is an old retired lady in Karlsruhe that really read the book.) What we have more and more of is this logic of how you presuppose the experience of the whole. And I also play this game. Now, I will reveal something to you (My God! Let's go to the end in this *Lingua Franca* territory!): often I don't have time to read the books about which I write. I will not tell you which ones. More and more (My God! This is a horrible thing to say!) I rely on summaries like *Cliffs Notes*. One English version of *Cliffs Notes* (it has a different name over there) is for me the ultimate sublime; it's a *Cliffs Notes* version of the Bible. At the end of the book, you get a description of the characters, and it says, "God, an old, omnipotent but jealous gentleman; Christ, a young gentleman." It's wonderful! So my idea is that the ultimate dream would be to write a *Cliffs Notes* summary of a non-existent story. You go directly to the *Cliffs Notes*, and if reactions to the *Cliffs Notes* volume are good, *then* you write the work. This would be interpassivity. I played an interpassive game in one of my lectures, for example, when I started with, "Let's recapitulate," and then I recapitulated something. Unfortunately, again, far from being a joke, this is part of our rhythm. There are already books that are written as if they are their own *Cliffs Notes*. For example, aren't a lot of the psychological self-help manuals often written precisely as their own recapitulation? So, again, I think that there is something crucial in this about how today's society functions.

Q. Are there any criticisms or misunderstandings of your work that you'd like to take issue with at this time?

A. Ah, that's a nice question! Let me try to answer this one in a very precise way. Maybe I am partially responsible for one misperception, so this is a self-criticism. My fundamental interest is and always has been a philosophical one: to re-actualize a certain philosophy of subjectivity as also the strongest emancipatory potential for feminism and for everything. What hurts me is that much of my so-called popularity depends much more on dirty jokes, popular culture, and a little bit of politics, and the philosophical aspect is overlooked. For example, take *The Ticklish Subject*. If you were to ask me which chapters I favor, I'd say the first two. These are the only two chapters that I really enjoyed writing. The one about how to save Kantian subjectivity from Heideggerian criticism, and the Hegel chapter. These are the ones I really enjoyed writing. There is another aspect in which I'm dissatisfied with myself, and this may surprise you. There is a certain cliché about intellectuals who pretend to read high culture but who privately read pornography, comics, detective novels; with me it's the opposite. I cannot survive without music; I always work with music, with loud music. I cannot survive without five or six hours of chamber music per day. What really frustrates me is (and I acknowledge my limits; I realize that I already write about too many topics) that I simply don't know enough to write about music. So, I'm traumatized: Why can't I write a nice essay on chamber music? I tried, but it's half success, half failure, but it's the closest I've come to it. It's not about Wagner; Wagner is more about ideologies. It's what I was doing in *The Plague of Fantasies* about Schumann. You can see my limits there. I can go to a certain point and cannot go further. My big dream is to take something like, say, Bach's violin sonatas, or the usual fashionable pieces like Beethoven's late string quartets, and to write a nice analysis of them, but I'm unable to do it. This is what really frustrates me.

Nevertheless, instead of complaining, let me end on a positive note. I'm not the kind of guy who says, "I have the ideas of a genius but I'm totally misunderstood." Let me admit to something, partially in contrast to what I just said: the nice surprise that I've experienced again and again is the extent to which there is out there an intelligent public who knows when my work is good and when it's not. What do I mean by this? The simple, most superficial criteria. Let's take *The Ticklish Subject*. It's a pretty difficult book—fewer jokes than usual, a thick book. At Verso, they were very skeptical about it. Let's take another book of mine that is much more into this toilet stuff and obscenities: *The Plague of Fantasies*. To put it in old-fashioned, almost reactionary terms, doesn't it restore your faith in the spiritual potential of humanity that *The Ticklish Subject* is selling much better than *The Plague of Fantasies* with all its obscenities, the German toilets, and so on? I'm pleasantly surprised that there is a public that knows how to appreciate it and that doesn't fall for the cheap, obscene tricks I use now and then. So the books that I consider really good, like *Tarrying with the Negative* and *The Ticklish Subject*, are also the books that are selling the best. It's a surprise, because publishers are idiots; they always ask me to write another cheap, obscene book. I try to tell them that people are not such idiots. So, this is a good surprise. Now, I *was* surprised and skeptical about *The*

Ticklish Subject. I had to blackmail, to threaten the editors at Verso. They really didn't want to publish it. They said, "Who will buy a four hundred-page book? Why don't you add a little bit more obscenity and make it shorter?" Yet, it's my best-selling book. My God! It's incredible how stupid publishers are. Again and again I discover this. In spite of all this commercialization, I have an old-fashioned, naive, trust—an Enlightenment trust, almost—in people. No! Most people are not idiots. They do know when you are bluffing. You know the saying: "You can deceive some people all the time, but you cannot deceive all people all the time." You can have short-lived successes, but in the long term people do guess. So instead of playing the game of complaining that I'm totally misunderstood, I would rather conclude by thanking the public. I am *well* understood. I have nothing to complain about.

Index

201